Incredible Cuisine

with Chef Jean-Pierre Brehier

Incredible Cuisine

with Chef Jean-Pierre Brehier

Time-Life Books
Alexandria, Virginia

Time-Life Books ia a division of
TIME LIFE INC.

TIME-LIFE CUSTOM PUBLISHING
Vice President and Publisher: Terry Newell
Associate Publisher: Teresa Hartnett
Vice President of Sales and Marketing: Neil Levin
Director of Special Sales: Liz Ziehl
Director of New Product Development: Quentin McAndrew
Project Manager: Jennifer M. Lee
Managing Editor: Donia Ann Steele
Director of Design: Christopher Register
Production Manager: Carolyn Bounds
Quality Assurance Manager: James D. King

Book Design: Ph D
Illustrations: Ann Field

First printing. Printed in U.S.A.

TIME-LIFE is a trademark of Time Warner Inc. U.S.A.

Library of Congress Cataloging-in-Publication Data

Incredible Cuisine with Chef Jean-Pierre Brehier
        p. cm.
    Includes index.
    ISBN 0-7835-4946-6
    I. Cookery. I. Time-Life Books. II. Title.
    TX714.B737 1997   97-22427
    641.5—dc21   CIP

Books produced by Time-Life Custom Publishing are available
at special bulk discount for promotional and premium use.
Custom adaptations can also be created to meet your specific
marketing goals. Call 1-800-323-5255.

dedication

I would like to dedicate this beautiful book to my mother, Yolande, whose personal recipe for success is to always deliver your own very best. And to all my cooking class students, whose support and sense of humor made this book a reality.

contents

introduction

I know what you're thinking: "Incredible cuisine?" Only a professional chef at a four-star restaurant could turn out food that's incredible, right? Wrong! I believe from the heart that anyone can learn to cook and cook well. All it takes is a willingness to educate yourself about the basic concepts and techniques and a little patience.

For too long there has been a false mystique about cooking. All that fancy language and those complicated-looking recipes made people think that to cook well you had to be a member of some secret club, a club they could never belong to. That's just not true. I mean, come on folks! Cooking is not like rocket science. And it's not like tennis or golf or piano, or any of those activities where you need to be born with a special gift to be successful. I assure you that with the proper tools—and I'll give you those tools—you, too, can prepare incredible, four-star cuisine right in your own kitchen.

One of the most important tools I will give you is explanation. I will not only tell you what to do in each recipe, I will also tell you why you are doing it. I was lucky enough to learn my way around the kitchen from my Italian mother, a Cordon Bleu-trained chef who cooked all day long, with me at her feet. She always took the time to explain things, to tell me why she did what she did.

This is what I want to do for you. Soon you, too, will begin to feel comfortable in the kitchen, comfortable enough to experiment with foods, because you will have the confidence that comes from truly knowing what you are doing. Sure, these recipes will require that you do more than simply open a can. But when you understand the steps and when you know why you are doing each one, you will realize that they are not difficult. And I promise you, the results will more than make up for a little bit of effort.

The key, as it is with so many things, is education; you need to take just a little time to learn about different ingredients and how they work with one another. Study and practice food preparation techniques. Get in the habit of reading a recipe through, from beginning to end (and more than once!), before picking up a single ingredient. See how much easier it is when you understand the right tools to use. If you do all this and if you pay attention to the fundamentals, I am absolutely convinced you'll have the foundation you need to be able to cook just about anything—and to dazzle your friends and family with your skills.

respecting ingredients

Ingredients—Ingredients are everything! Learning about ingredients, about their unique properties, and understanding how to combine them are crucial to establishing the solid foundation I'm talking about. When you have that, boy—then you can go on and really have fun in the kitchen.

My mom used to say that you must respect ingredients, respect that which makes each thing what it is. You should know, for example, that a tomato should never be refrigerated. An onion must "sweat," or be cooked for 5 to 7 minutes until the sugar comes out and caramelizes, making the onion transparent. That basil should be thrown into a sauce only at the end of the cooking process because to simmer it for 45 minutes kills the flavor. Garlic should be cooked for only a few seconds. People who don't "understand" garlic may put it in a pan to sauté along with the onions. When I see that, I flinch. Just a few seconds after garlic begins cooking, its essence is released—and at that moment, the moment you smell the fragrance, you must immediately add the wet ingredients. Otherwise, the garlic will "perfume" your kitchen, when you really want it to "perfume" the tomatoes or whatever it is you're adding to the pan.

The other important thing to remember about ingredients is that you must use absolutely the best you can find. You cannot succeed in preparing a great dish if you use second-rate ingredients. For instance, to me there's no such thing as "cooking wine." If you can't drink it, you shouldn't cook with it. Believe me, it won't get any better as you cook with it; if anything, it will get worse!

being prepared

Another thing that's critical to a solid cooking foundation is being prepared. That means not only reading every recipe all the way through at least twice before you start, but also making sure you have the right ingredients and tools on hand, and that you do all your chopping and dicing first. I can't emphasize this enough! The French have an expression for it: *mis-en-place*, which means, "everything in readiness." Oh sure, I know many people don't like this part of cooking, but I think it's because they don't know how to do it right. If you have the proper tools, especially a good knife, and learn how to use them, your prep time will be quick and easy.

Being prepared means other things, too. It means making sure your pantry and refrigerator are always stocked with key ingredients that are essential to great cooking—especially homemade stocks, sauces, and pestos. Homemade stocks are the foundation for all good sauces and soups. Think of it this way: Making a sauce is like constructing a building. Without a strong foundation, without a great stock, you won't get very far. You build a sauce by putting one layer, or flavor, on top of the other. This is what builds dimension. A sauce like this will tantalize the taste buds. It will stay with you because it has depth. Without that, it would taste flat, like a monotone. Boring. I will teach you to make sauces that are not boring.

Of course, to have this ready supply of wonderful stocks and pestos at your disposal, you need to invest some time. But you need only set aside one day each month for preparing and freezing the basics, for simmering vegetables and chicken and beef for stock, for whirring together basil and oil and nuts for pesto. Oh, I can hear you now: I don't have that day to spend in the kitchen! But I bet if you really tried, you could find it, and you'll really enjoy it. Believe me, this small investment will pay off every time you cook, because when you've got a strong foundation, everything you make will taste better. Think of it this way, too: With a freezer full of sauces and pestos, you'll never again rush in at 6:00 p.m. on a Wednesday evening, scrambling to find something to cook for dinner. All you'll have to do is boil some water for pasta and defrost a Bolognese sauce or a cube or two of pesto from the ice cube tray. That's it! "Fast food"—but a lot more delicious, and nutritious, than anything you'd get from a takeout place.

cooking without fat

This brings me to one more point. If you've flipped through this book, you may be wondering why I have noted that most of these recipes are low-fat, yet I have not really emphasized this. That's because I do not think of this as a "low-fat cookbook"; I think of it as a cookbook filled with recipes for food that tastes good! This, after all, has been my primary concern: making food that tastes good. But, we do want to live to enjoy our food, right? So, I do reduce saturated fat wherever I can, but I'm not going to sacrifice taste. If I need a little fat, I'm going to use a little fat—I want to make sure every recipe is a 10. That's why I prefer to think of this simply as a cookbook where fats are not necessary because the food tastes better without them!

Does that surprise you? Let me explain. By now, we all know that a diet high in fat is bad for you. It clogs your arteries, plain and simple. But I bet you also think that fat adds flavor to food. Well, guess what? Over the past few years, I've discovered it's just the opposite. In many, many instances, fat hides flavor! It hides the delicate essences of the ingredients. It is a barrier to taste.

I cannot honestly tell you that I started cutting fat in my recipes just because it was the right thing to do. In fact, for 17 years butter and cream were key ingredients in the classic French cuisine I prepared at my restaurant, The Left Bank, in Fort Lauderdale. But about five years ago, my business started to slow down for the first time ever, and my customers told me it was because they were concerned about their health, concerned about fat, and that they were changing the way they were eating. To save my restaurant, I had to adapt my cuisine—and believe me, it wasn't easy.

I quickly discovered that fat does not necessarily add taste, it only provides texture. I spent many frustrating Saturday afternoons in the kitchen, trying to figure out how to replicate the texture of my recipes without using fat. Mama mia, there were some disasters! Among other things, I just couldn't figure out how to make a smooth sauce without butter. But eventually, I did it. I learned that evaporated skim milk, thickened with a little cornstarch, makes a very creamy sauce. I now use ground turkey instead of ground beef. And, in recipes that call for bacon, I use 97% fat-free smoked ham sautéed with a little onion. My recipes now feature lots of fruits and vegetables, poultry and fish, pastas and grains. My cuisine has evolved into a contemporary, Mediterranean style that uses very little fat, emphasizing flavor above everything else. And business is booming better than ever at The Left Bank!

I truly believe that everyday cooking does not have to be a chore and that learning to cook impressive, healthy, delicious meals need not take years of hard work. I'll show you the right way to cook. When you understand what you're doing, why you're doing it, and how to make the most of your ingredients, your dishes will become incredible! And, you'll have a ball making these recipes and even exploring and creating your own masterpieces. To me, that's what cooking should be—fun.

basic equipment

immersion blender

A must for every kitchen, this tall, narrow blender has a very sharp blade at the end. It can be inserted directly into a saucepan, transforming an ordinary vegetable soup into a wonderfully creamy dish. You can save a sauce that has "separated" by emulsifying it with this blender. It is also very useful for eliminating lumps.

food processor

This marvelous kitchen appliance chops, dices, grinds, and purées almost any food. I cannot imagine cooking without it! You really need only one medium-sized processor. However, if you are into kitchen gadgets like I am, you could also get a "mini-processor." These are great for chopping a couple of shallots or garlic cloves, or a few sprigs of fresh herbs. A coffee grinder is also wonderful for pulverizing things like cinnamon sticks, nutmeg, or tapioca pearls.

tongs

It's amazing how much I depend on my tongs; I would be totally lost without them. They are like an extension of my fingers. If you are a beginner, get spring-loaded stainless steel tongs, no longer than 12 inches.

whisks

You need only two basic styles: a "sauce whisk" for blending sauce and soup ingredients and a "balloon whisk" with pear-shaped thin wires, which allow you to incorporate air into cream or eggs for maximum fluffiness. Heavy-duty stainless steel whisks are best.

sieves

You should have two kinds of sieves: one with a fine mesh and one with a medium mesh. The coarse netting is useful for straining a stock, while the finer weave helps to create a silky texture when finishing a sauce. Again, I recommend that you buy the finest quality stainless steel sieves you can afford. They will last you a lifetime.

pots & pans

At my cooking demonstrations, people always want to know: Which brands of pots do I use and what are my feelings about nonstick? I love to use stainless steel pots, as they are nonreactive to most food. And although I disliked nonstick pans 15 years ago, I now swear by them. You should have one small and one medium sauté pan, a couple of medium-sized saucepans, and a large (about 14-quart) stockpot. A small rondeau (6-inch-deep Dutch oven) is also fantastic for risotto and pasta dishes.

cheese grater

I have "a thing" (or two) about the "grated Parmesan cheese" that comes in a can. Please, do yourself a favor and buy a quality cheese grater in stainless steel or heavy plastic. Trust me, after you use freshly grated Parmigiano-Reggiano on top of a steaming risotto, you will never return to those prepared products from a can!

zester

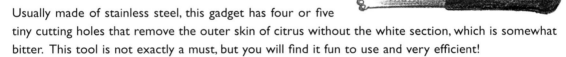

Usually made of stainless steel, this gadget has four or five tiny cutting holes that remove the outer skin of citrus without the white section, which is somewhat bitter. This tool is not exactly a must, but you will find it fun to use and very efficient!

"tabletop" mixer

This may be one of the most expensive small appliances you'll buy; prices range from $150 to $350. But if you plan on baking those wonderful cheesecakes or chiffon cakes, you'll thank me every time you use it! Buy yourself a very sturdy model, preferably one that comes with two bowls of at least $4^{1}/_{2}$ quarts, a whip, a paddle, and a dough hook.

spatula

Years ago, longer than I like to remember, I loved to spend time cooking in the kitchen with my mom. My job was to clean the mixing bowls. To this day, I still remember when my mom discovered the tool called the spatula. From then on, she would give me bowls to clean, but there was nothing left!

So furious was I (at the age of 5) that I would hide that "terrible tool" until she finally caught on and found 12 of them in the bottom of a kitchen drawer. Today I love spatulas, especially if they are heat-resistant. You can use them as you sauté fish, cook pancakes and, of course, scrape your mixing bowls. Just remember: If you ask your kids to "lick the bowls clean," leave something there!

knives

A knife may be the most important and often-used tool in your kitchen. Buy a high-quality knife and, if you take good care of it, it will last you a lifetime. An inexpensive one will become dull, lose its balance, and last only a couple of years. A good knife will feel very comfortable and balanced in your hand. I recommend that you buy a high-carbon stainless steel blade with a full tang (that is, the blade continues into the knife handle) that is as long as the entire handle.

Your starter kit should include:

A paring knife, approximately 3-inch blade, for peeling vegetables and fruit.

A boning knife, whose rigid 6- to 7-inch blade fits between the meat and bone or skin, making it easy to de-bone any poultry or meat.

An 8- to 10-inch chef's knife, for chopping, slicing, and dicing. Buy the best you can afford.

A slicer, a very thin knife with a 10-inch blade—a must for slicing cooked meat, poultry, and cured salmon without tearing the meat.

A steel, which does not sharpen your knives, but will keep them sharp if you use it regularly. If your knives become dull, you'll need a sharpening stone (or professional sharpening at a knife store).

pastry bags

A pastry bag can transform many preparations into masterpieces, easily and inexpensively. The best part is, you don't need to be an expert. You just need a 14- to 18-inch bag, plus two plain tips ($1/4$ to $1/2$ inch) and a few decorative tips.

a word on ingredients

olive oil

Always use extra-virgin olive oil. Never buy 100 percent pure olive oil, which is much less delicate and has hardly any olive flavor. A good extra-virgin olive oil usually has a deep green color. (However, the color is not always an indication of quality, since many producers press the leaves along with the olives to extract chlorophyll, which creates the deep green.) Next, look for a rich texture and a strong and very aromatic olive flavor. You will have to taste-test by comparing the flavors among a few small bottles. Stay away from an oil that is fatty, bitter, or bland with little or no olive flavor.

vinegar

I find that I use only a few different types of vinegar. When I want to add a soft and delicate flavor, I use a good red and a good white wine vinegar. (But don't confuse white vinegar and white wine vinegar—the white vinegar is wonderful for cleaning your windows and floors, but please, never use it in your food!) The rice-wine vinegar is usually very mild, perfect when you need just a slight hint of vinegar flavor. Apple-cider vinegar adds the beautiful and delicate fragrance of apple to any sauce. My favorite, which I use in so many of my recipes, is balsamic vinegar. This aromatic vinegar is aged for at least four years in oak, chestnut, ash, or cherry barrels, and can be aged for up to 50 years or more. Usually the longer it ages, the sweeter it becomes; in fact, in can reach a rich amber-color liquid that can be enjoyed as an after-dinner drink. For cooking, however, use the vinegars you find in the supermarket. They should be brilliant and clear but never cloudy. A good balsamic vinegar should have a sharp, pungent aftertaste.

herbs

I have this "thing" about dried herbs found in bottles or tins at the supermarket! I do not like them! Every jar I open smells the same to me; you may as well use hay for flavoring. So, except when you are making dried bread crumbs, try to always use fresh herbs. And, if your market does not have them, buy some seeds and try to grow them in your kitchen window. It is easy and so rewarding! When your basil gets particularly bushy, cut it all before you lose it, make a pesto, and freeze it.

garlic

If you have read my recipes or have watched my television show, you probably know that I love garlic. I can't help it; I was born with it. My mother uses it everywhere—and I do mean everywhere. Everywhere but dessert! Try to choose heads of garlic with tight, papery skin and firm cloves. I never use a garlic press, since I find it easier to just smack the garlic between a cutting board and the flat side of my chef's knife. The papery skin will slip right off and all you need to do is chop it. Remember, don't overcook garlic, as it may become bitter.

phyllo pastry

I have used phyllo (or filo) pastry in several recipes, even though it can be somewhat difficult to work with at times. One of the first, and most critical, steps for success: Let it defrost at room temperature for at least 6 hours before you use it. Work with it very slowly and carefully; in fact, if you're in a hurry, you should skip any recipe involving phyllo. It is a great dough to use because it is low in fat, and I love the end result—a crispy, light, and very flavorful dough.

evaporated milk

Evaporated skim milk is a wonderful ingredient not just because it has no fat, but also—and most importantly—because it does not overpower the delicate flavors of a dish the way heavy cream can. Because it is thinner, it allows ingredients to retain their integrity. But be careful: If you bring evaporated skim milk to a boil, your sauce or soup could "break" on you. If this happens, just strain the entire mixture and, using an immersion blender, blend it for a few minutes, and it will regain its smooth texture.

parmigiano-reggiano

There are certain ingredients that are not replaceable in my kitchen, and I am happy to tell you that whenever I call for Parmesan cheese in any recipe, I mean "Parmigiano-Reggiano." The taste and consistency of this cheese is matchless. If you can't locate it in your supermarket, ask for it. Or, any Italian market worthy of the name will have "Parmigiano-Reggiano."

tomatoes

A truly ripe tomato is certainly hard to find in any market. But when you do find it—incredible! I love a vine-ripened tomato that actually smells and tastes like a tomato. With a kiss of extra-virgin olive oil, a chiffonade of fresh basil, and a couple drops of balsamic vinegar—what else can I say? When buying tomatoes select the ripest ones, making sure they are not too soft. Never refrigerate them, as it will interfere with the flavor and texture. And, when you cook tomatoes, be sure to peel and seed them.

97% fat-free smoked ham

The secret to using smoked ham, instead of bacon, is to cut the ham into small cubes and sauté the cubes in a touch of extra-virgin olive oil. This creates a wonderful texture and extracts some of the smoked flavors. So, if you need $1/4$ cup of smoked ham cubes for a recipe, go to the deli counter and order 1 slice of 97% fat-free smoked ham $1/4$ inch thick, cut it julienne (long strips), and then dice it to $1/4$-inch squares.

hors d'oeuvres

I like to think of hors d'oeuvres as little pieces of art, shaped or filled or rolled, one by one, into beautiful and delicious mouthfuls that welcome your guests and whet their appetites for the food yet to come. I love to serve them with Champagne or a crisp Chardonnay.

Hors d'oeuvres are labor-intensive, there's no doubt about it. But I have given you recipes for two hors d'oeuvres that are quick and simple—the Spicy Sea Scallops on Skewers (page 22) and the Barbecue Shrimp on Skewers (page 23), both of which are perfect for a party because you can make them ahead and just finish off the cooking as your guests arrive.

You should not prepare these hors d'oeuvres when you're in a hurry. In fact, you should skip the hors d'oeuvres altogether, rather than try to make them fast. But when you do have time, have some fun with a recipe like the Cherry Tomato & Crab Salad Bouchées (page 24). Your efforts will pay off because the presentation is just beautiful— everyone will think those little tomatoes are so cute!

Spicy Sea Scallops on Skewers

THIS is the absolute perfect recipe for a party because it's so easy, and you can make it ahead. Just be careful not to overdo it when you are searing the scallops. As your guests are arriving, pop these in the oven to finish the cooking, and voilà! If you don't have the skewers to serve them on, you can use toothpicks.

1 teaspoon paprika

¹/₄ teaspoon cayenne pepper (optional)

1 tablespoon extra-virgin olive oil

24 sea scallops (20 to 30 count), patted dry

several endive tips, for garnish

Thai Curry Sauce (recipe on page 246)

Mix the paprika and cayenne together and dredge the scallops in the mixture.

In a nonstick skillet, heat the olive oil. Sear the scallops for 2 minutes on each side. Insert a bamboo skewer into the middle of each scallop and arrange the scallops on a serving platter with endive tips. Place a glass bowl in the center of the platter and fill it with the Thai Curry Sauce.

Barbecue Shrimp on Skewers

WHAT great party hors d'oeuvres! Grill or poach the shrimp ahead of time and finish the cooking once your guests have arrived. Serve with my Barbecue Sauce or, if you want, your own favorite bottled sauce. Just make sure the flavor isn't too strong; you don't want it to overpower the shrimp.

24 medium to large shrimp (20 to 30 count), peeled and deveined

2 cups Barbecue Sauce (recipe on page 244)

On a hot grill, cook the shrimp until opaque all the way through, about 3 minutes. (Or you can poach them in water with a few bay leaves and black peppercorns.)

Spear the shrimp with bamboo skewers. Serve on a platter with the Barbecue Sauce in the center, so your guests can dip them in the sauce and enjoy!

Canapés of Chicken & Sun-Dried Tomato Mousse

YOU would think this recipe would be complicated, but it's actually so simple to make! The key to success: Do not refrigerate the chicken, or the mousse won't be smooth when processed.

makes 24 canapés

1 whole chicken, 2 to 2^1/$_2$ pounds

^{1}/$_2$ cup boysenberry or raspberry jam

^{1}/$_4$ cup heavy cream

^{1}/$_4$ cup sun-dried tomatoes, reconstituted in water (not oil)

salt & freshly ground black pepper to taste

24 crackers for serving

6 black olives, cut into 24 slices

snipped fresh chives for garnish

Preheat oven to 450°F.

Place the chicken in a roasting pan on the center rack of the oven. Cook until the juices run clear, approximately 35 minutes. Allow it to cool at room temperature for 1 hour.

Remove the skin and take the meat off the bones. Place the meat into a food processor. Add the jam, cream, sun-dried tomatoes, salt, and pepper. Process until very smooth. It should have the consistency of a thick paste. To improve the consistency and create a very smooth texture, strain through a fine sieve into a bowl. (Use a rubber spatula to press it through the sieve.)

Cool for at least 2 hours in the refrigerator.

Using a pastry bag fitted with a decorative star tip, pipe enough mousse to cover each cracker. Garnish each with a slice of black olive and a few snipped chives.

Cherry Tomato & Crab Salad Bouchées

makes 24 bite-sized tomatoes

24 cherry tomatoes, washed and dried

^{1}/$_4$ pound lump crabmeat

^{1}/$_4$ cup finely diced apples

3 tablespoons finely diced red onions

2 tablespoons small capers

2 tablespoons sour cream

1 teaspoon Dijon mustard

salt & freshly ground black pepper to taste

Slice off the tops of the tomatoes and save. Using a small spoon or a small melon ball cutter, remove the inside of each tomato. Place the tomatoes cut side down on a paper towel to dry.

In the meantime, make the salad. Mix all the ingredients in a large glass bowl. Using a very small spoon, fill the tomatoes and place the tops back on.

Cured Salmon & Cilantro Cream Cheese Canapés

THE secret to both of these good-looking and good-tasting hors d'oeuvres is the pastry bag. If you've never tried one, don't be afraid; it's so easy to use!

makes 24 canapés

Cream Cheese:

8 ounces low-fat cream cheese, softened

2 tablespoons snipped fresh chives

$^1/_4$ teaspoon salt

$^1/_4$ teaspoon freshly ground black pepper

Canapés:

24 very thin slices cured salmon

24 thin slices pumpernickel bread

24 small sprigs fresh dill

In a glass bowl, blend all the Cream Cheese ingredients. Transfer to a pastry bag fitted with a decorative star tip.

Cut the bread with a cookie cutter into bite-sized pieces.

Pipe about 1 tablespoon of cream cheese onto the pumpernickel pieces. Roll each slice of salmon very tightly and place carefully in the center of the cream cheese.

Decorate with a small sprig of fresh dill.

Nouvelle Potato Bites Stuffed with Goat Cheese, Sour Cream & Caviar

makes 24 bite-sized appetizers

24 small creamer potatoes

$^1/_2$ cup sour cream

3 tablespoons soft goat cheese

2 tablespoons snipped fresh chives

1 ounce caviar

8 whole chives for decoration, cut into 1-inch pieces

Peel the potatoes and trim them with a paring knife down to the desired bite size. Trim the bottoms flat. Using a small melon ball cutter, remove just enough potato from the top to create a small cavity.

Boil the potatoes until tender and cooked all the way through. Place the potatoes upside down on paper towels and set in the refrigerator for 2 hours.

In the meantime, mix the sour cream and goat cheese in a bowl and blend in the snipped chives. Cool for 30 minutes.

Transfer the cheese mixture to a pastry bag fitted with a decorative star tip and fill the cavities of the potatoes. Top with approximately $^1/_2$ teaspoon of caviar and decorate with 2 chive pieces.

Gravad Lox
(Cured Salmon)

YOU'LL find this an extremely, *extremely* easy recipe to prepare. Just be sure to leave yourself enough time if you are serving it at a party or a brunch because the salmon must be refrigerated for at least 2 days. You'll also need a high-quality knife to get the slices as thin as they should be. But oh, how your friends will thank you: Cured salmon, bagels, and cream cheese? Forget about it! They'll eat it up, no problem.

makes 20 to 30 appetizers

1 salmon fillet (skin on)
3 tablespoons brandy
2 cups fresh dill leaves
$^{1}/_{2}$ cup sea salt
$^{1}/_{2}$ cup sugar

Using needle-nosed pliers, remove the bones that run down the center of the fillet, being careful to pull out every one. You will find as many as 30 of them. Rub the brandy on both sides of the salmon.

With the salmon skin side down, cover the top completely with dill, then spread on the salt and sugar evenly to coat the dill. Wrap the fillet tightly in plastic wrap.

Place a baking sheet on top of the salmon, then place two heavy cans (they should weigh approximately the same as a brick) on top of the baking sheet. Refrigerate for at least 2 days.

At the sink, discard the liquid that drains off of the salmon. Wash off the excess salt and sugar, being careful that you do not remove the dill.

Slice the salmon as thinly as you possibly can, starting at the head end. (The tail is usually dry and only good for pasta or a cured salmon mousse.)

Reggiano Parmesan & Goat Cheese Puffs

TO get the fluffiest, most delicious cheese puffs, it's very, very important that you follow these directions carefully. And if it doesn't work the first time, keep trying—it's worth it! Here's a tip: when piping the dough, use a circular motion to make nice even puffs.

1 cup 2% milk

6 tablespoons unsalted butter

1 pinch salt

1 cup all-purpose flour

5 large eggs

1/2 cup freshly grated Reggiano Parmesan cheese

1/2 cup goat cheese

2 dashes Tabasco sauce

Preheat oven to 425°F.

Spray a baking sheet with nonstick cooking spray.

In a saucepan, scald the milk, add the butter and salt. Remove the pan from the heat and add the flour all at once, to avoid lumps.

Using a wooden spoon, mix vigorously so the mixture gathers together. Return the pan to medium heat and continue to mix vigorously until the mixture comes away from the sides and starts to dry out (only 1 minute is necessary).

Transfer the dough to a stainless steel or glass bowl, or to the bowl of an electric mixer fitted with a paddle. Add 1 egg at a time, always waiting until the egg is incorporated before adding another. After all the eggs are incorporated, add both cheeses and the Tabasco.

Transfer the mixture to a pastry bag fitted with a star tip. Pipe puffs—about 2 tablespoons of dough for each—onto the prepared baking sheet, spacing them 2 inches apart.

Bake for 25 minutes without opening the oven door. Serve immediately for fluffy and moist cheese puffs.

incredible cuisine

appetizers

I am never surprised when a patron at my restaurant orders three or four appetizers, rather than an entrée. I sometimes feel the same way when I eat out: All the appetizers sound so tempting, I can't decide which to get! So I occasionally solve my dilemma by making a meal of them, which gives me the best of both worlds. I get a lot of different taste sensations, but the portions are small enough so that I still have room for dessert.

If you're like me, when you entertain at home you want your guests to be as excited about the appetizer as they are about the main course. Then you must try the phenomenal Turkey Cannelloni Wrapped in Phyllo Pastry (page 34) or the Shrimp, Scallops & Salmon Strudel (page 56)—very, very impressive and perfect for company.

But remember: Preparing appetizers can be just as involved as preparing entrées. That's why you must read each recipe at least twice before you begin, so that you understand all the steps. Chop all the ingredients before you start using the first sauté pan. Think carefully about your menu because you probably don't want to pair a complicated appetizer with a complicated main course (unless you'd like to spend days in the kitchen, which is okay, too!).

Turkey Cannelloni Wrapped in Phyllo Pastry with Roasted Bell Pepper Coulis

J UST thinking of this dish makes my mouth water! I love it when the cannelloni first comes out of the oven with the cheese oozing out.

makes 6 servings

2 tablespoons extra-virgin olive oil

$^1/_2$ cup diced yellow onions

$^1/_2$ cup diced celery heart

1 pound ground extra-lean turkey breast

$^1/_4$ pound wild mushrooms such as shiitake, oyster, or cremini

2 tablespoons chopped fresh garlic

about 3$^1/_2$ pounds ripe tomatoes, peeled, seeded, chopped, and drained, to make 4 cups

2 tablespoons tomato paste

1 tablespoon chopped fresh thyme leaves

1 teaspoon chopped fresh oregano leaves

salt & freshly ground black pepper to taste

12 sheets phyllo pastry

2 tablespoons extra-virgin olive oil or olive oil cooking spray

4 ounces nonfat cream cheese

Roasted Bell Pepper Coulis (recipe on page 253)

In a sauté pan, heat the olive oil. Add the onions and sweat them for 2 to 3 minutes. Add the celery and cook for 1 more minute. Add the turkey and sauté until golden brown.

Stir in the wild mushrooms and garlic. Sauté for 2 minutes. When the garlic becomes fragrant, add the tomatoes, tomato paste, thyme, and oregano. Adjust the seasoning with salt and pepper and let simmer slowly for 30 minutes.

Refrigerate for 2 to 3 hours.

Preheat oven to 400°F.

Pull out 3 sheets of pastry at a time, keeping the rest of the dough covered with a slightly dampened towel to keep it from drying out. Place the 3 sheets in front of you and brush the first sheet very lightly with olive oil or spray with olive oil cooking spray. Spoon about 3 to 4 ounces of refrigerated turkey mixture almost to the edge of the first sheet. Spread about 1 ounce of cream cheese on top of the turkey. Start rolling the dough slowly and carefully until you reach half of the sheet. Fold each side over the roll and continue to roll the entire sheet. Repeat the same procedure for the remaining 2 sheets. Set the cannelloni on a nonstick baking sheet, rolling 9 more cannelloni, working with 3 sheets of phyllo at a time, as above. Brush the tops lightly with butter or olive oil and bake for 7 to 10 minutes, until the phyllo is a nice golden brown. Serve immediately with the Roasted Bell Pepper Coulis.

Shrimp with Bourbon Barbecue Sauce

I made this wonderful dish on the Today Show and it generated a phenomenal response! I am sure this recipe will become one of your favorites.

makes 4 servings

16 jumbo shrimp (15 count)

2 tablespoons extra-virgin olive oil, divided

2 shallots, chopped fine

1 red bell pepper, cut into tiny dice

2 scallions, sliced diagonally

$^1/_2$ cup Chardonnay or other full-bodied, dry white wine

$^1/_4$ cup bourbon

$^1/_2$ cup Barbecue Sauce (recipe on page 244)

$^1/_4$ cup evaporated skim milk

1 tablespoon cornstarch mixed with 2 tablespoons water

Peel and devein the shrimp.

In a saucepan, heat 1 tablespoon of the olive oil and when hot, sweat the shallots. Add the peppers and scallions; sauté for a couple of minutes. Pour in the wine and bourbon. Let reduce until half remains in the pan. Add the Barbecue Sauce. Stir in the evaporated milk and cornstarch mixture; do not boil.

In the meantime, in a sauté pan, heat the remaining 1 tablespoon olive oil and cook the shrimp for 2 to 3 minutes on each side.

Spoon enough sauce onto the dinner plates to cover the bottom and place the shrimp on top. Serve with barley, rice, or your favorite pasta.

Shrimp à l'Américaine

YES, you read it right: You should cook the shrimp shells when preparing this sauce; they are full of wonderful flavor and fragrance.

makes 4 servings

2 cups Chardonnay or other full-bodied, dry white wine

20 to 25 saffron threads

1 tablespoon extra-virgin olive oil

16 large shrimp (16 to 20 count), peeled and deveined (save the shells)

2 shallots, minced

¼ cup sweet sherry

¼ cup brandy

2 tablespoons tomato purée

½ cup evaporated skim milk

1 tablespoon cornstarch mixed with 1 tablespoon water

2 tablespoons snipped fresh chives

1 dash Tabasco sauce

salt & freshly ground black pepper to taste

In a small saucepan, combine the wine and saffron. Cook over medium heat for 15 minutes to reduce.

In a skillet, heat the olive oil and add the shrimp. Sauté on both sides for about 2 to 3 minutes. Remove the shrimp and set aside. Add the shallots and shrimp shells to the skillet and sauté for 2 minutes. Stir in the sherry, brandy, and tomato purée and let reduce for 2 minutes. Add the evaporated milk and the saffron-infused wine. Stir in the milk and cornstarch mixture, but do not bring to a boil.

Strain the sauce through a fine sieve and adjust the seasoning with the chives, a dash of Tabasco sauce, and salt and pepper.

Return the shrimp to the pan. Serve with linguine or fettuccine.

Mango & Red Onion Shrimp Salad with Grapefruit & Lime Vinaigrette

S ERVE this refreshing salad in a hollowed-out, vine-ripened tomato on a bed of mixed baby greens.

makes 6 servings

2 quarts water

$^1/_2$ celery stalk, cut into large pieces

8 whole black peppercorns

1 bay leaf

1 lime, cut in half

1$^1/_2$ pounds medium to large shrimp (21 to 25 count), shells on

1 mango cut into $^1/_4$-inch dice

1 small red onion, minced fine

grapefruit & lime vinaigrette

juice of 1 lime

1 tablespoon apple-cider vinegar

$^1/_2$ cup freshly squeezed grapefruit juice

2 tablespoons chopped fresh cilantro or Italian parsley

$^1/_4$ cup extra-virgin olive oil

salt & freshly ground black pepper to taste

Bring the water to a boil in a saucepan. Add the celery, peppercorns, and bay leaf. Squeeze the lime juice into the water and add the whole lime. When the water comes to a boil, reduce heat, cover, and let simmer for 10 minutes.

Raise the heat to boil again and add the shrimp. Cover and turn the heat off. Leave the pan on the stove for 5 minutes. Remove the shrimp and rinse in an ice-water bath to immediately stop the cooking process.

Peel and devein the shrimp and keep in the refrigerator until the vinaigrette is completed.

In a glass bowl large enough to hold the shrimp, mix all the ingredients for the vinaigrette.

To serve, add the cooked shrimp, the mangoes and red onions to the vinaigrette. Toss to coat everything well, cover, and refrigerate for at least 2 hours. Just before serving, toss again.

Mussels in a Saffron & Cilantro Bisque

THIS recipe takes me back, oh, 25 or 30 years, to my days in the sidewalk cafés on the French Riviera. I love mussels, especially if I can find the little farm-raised ones, since they usually have no sand in them. The key ingredient is saffron, which you must cook in wine to extract its aromatic fragrance and beautiful golden color. The Pernod adds a licorice flavor to this outstanding dish; if Pernod is not available, you can add a little anisette.

makes 4 servings

1 1/2 cups Chardonnay or other full-bodied, dry white wine

20 saffron threads, approximately

1 tablespoon extra-virgin olive oil

2 pounds mussels, scrubbed

2 shallots, chopped

1 tablespoon chopped fresh garlic

1/2 cup evaporated milk

about 1 3/4 pounds ripe tomatoes, peeled, seeded, and chopped, to make 2 cups

1 tablespoon Pernod liqueur

1 tablespoon chopped fresh cilantro

1 teaspoon cornstarch mixed with 2 tablespoons water

salt & ground white pepper to taste

In a saucepan, combine the wine and the saffron. Cook over medium heat until only 1/4 cup remains, about 15 minutes.

In a Dutch oven or soup kettle, heat the olive oil, then add the mussels and shallots. Cover and cook 3 to 4 minutes. Add the garlic and when fragrant, add the wine-and-saffron reduction. Add the evaporated milk and when hot, add the tomatoes, Pernod, cilantro, and cornstarch mixture.

Season with salt and white pepper. Divide the opened mussels and sauce equally onto 4 serving plates. Discard any mussels that have not opened.

Shrimp Sambuca

THIS is a phenomenal recipe! It is also special to me because it is one of my oldest recipes—and the first one that I prepared on television. Since then, I must have made it about a thousand times, but it is still, without a doubt, one of my favorites. I have eliminated the cream and butter with no loss of flavor or texture, thanks to the evaporated milk and cornstarch mixture. Just be sure to add the cornstarch mixture a bit at a time.

makes 4 appetizer servings

1 tablespoon extra-virgin olive oil

1 1/2 pounds large shrimp (16 to 20 count), peeled and deveined

2 medium shallots, very finely chopped

2 tablespoons dry vermouth

2 tablespoons sambuca liqueur

1 large ripe tomato, peeled, seeded, and diced 1/4 inch

salt & freshly ground black pepper to taste

1/2 cup evaporated skim milk

1 tablespoon cornstarch mixed with 1 tablespoon water

In a skillet large enough to hold the shrimp without crowding, heat the olive oil. When hot, add the shrimp and sauté for 2 to 3 minutes. Turn the shrimp over, add the shallots and sweat them for 1 minute, making sure not to burn them. Add the vermouth and sambuca and let reduce by half. Add the tomatoes, salt, and pepper to taste and cook for 2 more minutes. Stir in the evaporated milk and the cornstarch mixture. Heat without bringing it to a boil.

Serve immediately.

incredible cuisine

Shrimp with Ginger-Infused Carrot Jus

THIS is a very elegant appetizer. If you don't have a juicer, you should buy one! In the meantime, you can buy the carrot juice at any health food store and at most grocery stores. You can thicken the juice with arrowroot or cornstarch if you don't have tapioca.

makes 4 appetizer servings

16 large shrimp (16 to 20 count)
1 tablespoon extra-virgin olive oil
sprigs of fresh tarragon for garnish

Peel and devein the shrimp. In a sauté pan, heat the olive oil and cook the shrimp on both sides for 2 to 3 minutes. Pour enough carrot jus into each of 4 deep soup plates to cover the bottom. Place the shrimp on top and garnish with fresh tarragon.

Serve with rice pilaf or couscous.

ginger-infused carrot jus

12 medium carrots
one 1-inch piece fresh ginger
$1/4$ cup orange juice concentrate
1 teaspoon lime juice
1 tablespoon ground tapioca powder*
1 tablespoon fresh tarragon, chopped

Peel and juice the carrots and ginger with a regular juicer.

In a stainless steel pot, combine the carrot and ginger juices with the orange juice concentrate, lime juice, tapioca, and tarragon. Bring to a boil and reduce heat to medium low. Cook for 15 minutes.

* If you cannot find tapioca powder, you can make it by using regular tapioca. Just grind the tapioca pearls in a coffee grinder until it becomes the consistency of flour. You may also substitute with arrowroot.

Crab, Salmon & Scallop Cakes with Papaya, Mango & Pineapple Relish

I'VE tasted thousands of crab cakes, but none quite as delicious as these. The egg substitute is a phenomenal binding ingredient that doesn't add any fat. If you're going to try only one appetizer in this book, make it this one. Your guests will just love it.

makes 6 cakes

8 ounces salt-free saltine crackers

2 ounces whole-wheat crackers

3 egg substitutes

1/4 cup chopped fresh cilantro leaves

3 garlic cloves

1 tablespoon chopped fresh ginger

1 dash Tabasco sauce OR 1/4 Scotch bonnet chile (stem removed, seeded, and quartered)

salt & ground white pepper to taste

8 ounces salmon, cut into 1/2-inch cubes

8 ounces sea scallops, cut into 1/2-inch cubes

8 ounces jumbo lump crabmeat

1/2 green bell pepper, finely diced

1/2 red bell pepper, finely diced

1/2 yellow bell pepper, finely diced

1 tablespoon extra-virgin olive oil

Papaya, Mango & Pineapple Relish (recipe on page 252)

Preheat oven to 350°F.

Using your food processor, make crumbs with the saltine and whole-wheat crackers but keep them in separate bowls.

In a food processor, combine the egg substitutes, cilantro, garlic, ginger, Tabasco (or chile pepper), and salt and white pepper to taste. Mix until all the ingredients are liquid.

In a large glass or stainless steel bowl, combine the salmon and scallops plus the egg mixture. Mix well until the seafood is coated with egg. Add the whole-wheat cracker crumbs, mix again, and then carefully fold in the crabmeat.

Divide into six balls. Form into cakes that are approximately 3 inches in diameter and 1 inch thick. Roll in the saltine crumbs until totally coated.

In a nonstick, ovenproof sauté pan, heat the olive oil. Sauté the cakes until golden brown on one side. Turn them over and bake in the oven for 10 minutes. Serve with the Papaya, Mango & Pineapple Relish.

Crab-Stuffed Shrimp with Tomato & Cucumber Relish

YOU should pick the largest shrimp you can find for this simple but impressive appetizer. I like to use a small ice-cream scoop to stuff the shrimp, which you could certainly do in advance. The Tomato & Cucumber Relish is a perfect complement.

makes 4 appetizer servings

16 jumbo shrimp (15 count or larger), peeled

1 ounce whole-wheat crackers

2 egg substitutes

1/4 cup chopped fresh ginger

1 garlic clove

1/4 small Scotch bonnet chile pepper OR a dash of Tabasco sauce

8 ounces jumbo lump crabmeat

1 tablespoon extra-virgin olive oil

2 cups Tomato & Cucumber Relish (recipe on page 251)

Crumble the whole-wheat crackers into fine crumbs, using a food processor. Set aside. In the food processor, combine the egg substitutes, ginger, garlic, and chile pepper, or Tabasco. Process until all the ingredients are liquid.

In a large glass or stainless steel bowl, combine the crab-meat and the egg mixture. Mix carefully, but thoroughly.

Holding the shrimp flat on a cutting board, cut an opening with the point of a knife to create a pocket. Be careful to not cut all the way through. This process will allow you to devein the shrimp and create a cavity for the crab stuffing.

Stuff each shrimp with about 2 tablespoons of stuffing per shrimp. Set aside in the refrigerator for at least 1 to 2 hours while you prepare the relish.

In a sauté pan, heat the olive oil and when hot, carefully place the shrimp in the pan and sauté at medium heat for 2 to 3 minutes; cover and cook for 2 more minutes. Serve with the Tomato & Cucumber Relish.

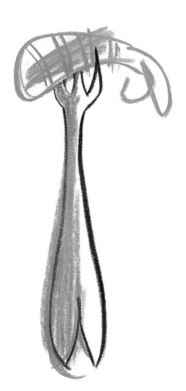

Wild Mushroom & Sun-Dried Tomato Brûlée in a Couscous Crust

THE correct tart mold—6 inches in diameter and $3/4$ inch high, with a removable bottom—is a must for this recipe.

makes 6 servings

- 2 cups cooked couscous
- 2 egg substitutes
- 2 tablespoons red bell pepper brunoise
- 1 teaspoon fresh tarragon, chopped

filling

- $1^{1}/_{2}$ cups milk
- 1 tablespoon extra-virgin olive oil
- 2 shallots, finely diced
- $^{1}/_{4}$ pound mixed wild mushrooms (such as shiitake, cremini, oyster), sliced
- 2 tablespoons sun-dried tomatoes not packed in oil (follow package directions to reconstitute the tomatoes), chopped very fine
- 1 tablespoon chopped fresh garlic
- 2 ounces mozzarella cheese, grated
- 4 eggs
- 1 teaspoon cornstarch mixed with 1 tablespoon water
- $^{1}/_{4}$ teaspoon grated nutmeg
- salt & ground white pepper to taste

To make couscous crust, mix all the ingredients in a bowl.

Using 4 individual tart molds with removable bottoms, spray the insides with a nonstick cooking spray. Divide the couscous into 4 equal amounts and press into the bottoms and sides of the molds.

Preheat oven to 375°F.

Begin heating the milk in a saucepan (do not boil).

In a sauté pan, heat the olive oil and when hot, add the shallots and sweat them for 1 minute. Add the mushrooms and sun-dried tomatoes. Cook for 2 to 3 minutes. Add the garlic and when fragrant, remove from heat immediately. Divide this mixture into 4 equal parts and spoon into the couscous-crusted tart molds. Sprinkle the cheese on top of the mushrooms.

To the hot milk, add the eggs, cornstarch mixture, and nutmeg. Adjust the seasoning with salt and white pepper. Cook over medium heat for 2 to 3 minutes.

Pour the milk mixture over the mushrooms in each mold. Bake for 10 to 12 minutes until the tops are nice and brown. Let the tarts rest for 15 minutes before serving.

Sea Scallops in a Whiskey, Tomato & Fennel Bisque

WHAT a very elegant and delicate appetizer! Be careful not to overcook the scallops; they should be translucent on the inside.

makes 6 servings

2 tablespoons extra-virgin olive oil, divided

2 shallots, minced

1 cup fennel bulb, cut into small $1/4$-inch cubes (save 2 tablespoons chopped leaves)

$1/4$ cup rice-wine vinegar

$1/2$ cup Chardonnay or other full-bodied, dry white wine

$1/4$ cup whiskey

$1^3/4$ pounds ripe tomatoes, peeled, seeded, and chopped, to make 2 cups

2 tablespoons tomato paste

1 cup Chicken Stock (recipe on page 240)

1 pound sea scallops (20 to 30 count)

$3/4$ cup evaporated skim milk

1 tablespoon cornstarch mixed with 2 tablespoons water

salt & freshly ground black pepper to taste

$3/4$ pound freshly cooked angel hair (cappellini) or other pasta

In a saucepan, heat 1 tablespoon of the olive oil over medium heat; add the shallots and sweat them for about 2 minutes. Add the fennel and sweat it for 2 minutes. Pour in the vinegar and let reduce until almost dry. Add the wine and whiskey and let reduce until half the liquid remains. Add the tomatoes, tomato paste, and stock. Cook for 15 minutes at very low heat.

In the meantime, in a large sauté pan, heat the remaining 1 tablespoon olive oil over medium to high heat. Add the scallops and cook until they are golden brown on both sides. Set aside while you finish the bisque.

In a blender, purée the tomato mixture until very smooth. For an even smoother consistency, strain through a fine sieve. Return the bisque to the saucepan. Add the evaporated milk, the cornstarch mixture, and the chopped fennel leaves. Heat but do not boil. Adjust the seasoning with salt and pepper.

To serve, pour approximately $1/2$ cup of bisque into each of 6 deep plates. Arrange the scallops all around the edge and place a mound of pasta in the middle.

whiskey

Stuffed & Roasted Bell Peppers with Turkey, Wild Mushrooms & Tomatoes

THE key to success with this recipe is to poach the peppers for at least 10 to 15 minutes before you stuff and bake them.

makes 4 servings

4 very nicely shaped red bell peppers

1 tablespoon extra-virgin olive oil

$\frac{1}{2}$ cup diced white onions

1 pound ground turkey breast meat

1 cup finely diced celery

$\frac{1}{2}$ green pepper, cut into brunoise ($\frac{1}{4}$ cup)

$\frac{1}{2}$ yellow pepper, cut into brunoise ($\frac{1}{4}$ cup)

3 pounds ripe tomatoes, peeled, seeded, and chopped, to make 3 cups

1 cup tomato purée

1 cup wild mushrooms, sliced

2 tablespoons minced fresh garlic

1 tablespoon chopped fresh thyme leaves

1 tablespoon chopped fresh rosemary leaves

salt & freshly ground black pepper to taste

Spiced Tomato & Basil Sauce (recipe on page 245)

Bring a pot of water to a boil. Cut the tops off the bell peppers and save. Discard the seeds and white ribs from inside, being careful not to break the peppers. Poach them in the boiling water until soft, about 10 minutes. Place the peppers cut side down on paper towels and allow to cool and drain.

In the meantime, in a large saucepan or Dutch oven, heat the olive oil. When hot, add the onions and cook until translucent, 3 to 4 minutes. Add the turkey and cook until a nice golden brown. Stir in the celery and the green and yellow peppers and cook for 5 minutes. Add the tomatoes, tomato purée, mushrooms, and garlic. Add the thyme and rosemary. Simmer slowly for 25 to 30 minutes. Adjust the seasoning with salt and pepper. Allow the mixture to cool for 30 minutes at room temperature for easier handling.

Preheat oven to 375°F.

Carefully spoon the turkey mixture into the peppers, filling almost to the top. Put the tops back on each pepper. Place the stuffed peppers on a nonstick baking sheet, cover with foil, and bake for 15 minutes.

Serve as an appetizer or a main course at lunch with the Spiced Tomato & Basil Sauce.

Zucchini & Yellow Squash Pancakes with Spiced Tomato & Basil Sauce

THESE little pancakes are so versatile: They make a wonderful side dish for chicken, beef, or even fish, but they also work beautifully as a vegetarian appetizer, served with the Spiced Tomato & Basil Sauce. The pancakes are easier to flip if you use a nonstick flat skillet or griddle for cooking them.

makes 6 servings

1 pound zucchini (about 2 medium)

$^1/_2$ pound yellow squash (about 2 small)

4 eggs

$^1/_2$ red bell pepper, cut into brunoise (tiny dice)

$^1/_4$ cup freshly grated Reggiano Parmesan cheese

1 tablespoon minced fresh garlic

1 tablespoon fresh thyme leaves, chopped

1 tablespoon freshly squeezed lime juice

$^1/_4$ teaspoon Tabasco sauce

2 tablespoons extra-virgin olive oil

Spiced Tomato & Basil Sauce (recipe on page 245)

Into a large glass bowl, coarsely grate the zucchini and yellow squash using the largest holes of your grater. Add the remaining ingredients except for the olive oil and stir to make a batter.

In a nonstick frying pan, nonstick griddle, or flat skillet, heat the olive oil. When hot, spoon approximately $^1/_3$ cup of batter in the pan and, using the back of a spoon, flatten it into a small cake. Repeat with the remaining batter.

Cook the pancakes until golden brown on both sides. Place the pancakes in the center of individual plates and ladle some Spiced Tomato & Basil Sauce around the edge.

Tomatoes Stuffed with Mushroom & Barley Risotto

A S a side dish, these tomatoes add a bit of glamour to any main course.

6 medium, vine-ripened tomatoes

1 quart water

$^3/_4$ cup barley

$^1/_2$ teaspoon salt

2 tablespoons extra-virgin olive oil

2 shallots, finely diced

$^1/_4$ cup finely diced onions

2 cups wild mushrooms (such as cremini, chantarelle, shiitake, or oyster), chopped

1 tablespoon minced fresh garlic

1 teaspoon chopped fresh thyme leaves

Roasted Bell Pepper Coulis (recipe on page 253)

If you are comfortable with taking the skin off the tomato, go right ahead. Poach them in hot water for 10 to 15 seconds. Remove the peeling skin. Cut the tops off the tomatoes and reserve. Using a small spoon or a melon ball cutter, empty the insides of the tomatoes (reserve the pulp for stocks or soup). Place the tomatoes cut side down on paper towels and allow to drain.

Heat the water, barley, and salt and cook for approximately 45 minutes (mixing with a wooden spoon every 10 minutes), or until barley is about 95 percent cooked.

While the barley is cooking, heat the olive oil in a sauté pan. When hot, add the shallots and onions until light golden brown. Add the mushrooms and sauté for 2 minutes to soften. Add the garlic and thyme.

Preheat oven to 375°F.

Drain the barley and, in a glass bowl, mix the barley with the sautéed mushrooms. Fill each tomato with the barley and mushroom mixture and bake for 15 minutes.

Shrimp, Scallops & Salmon Strudel with a Champagne Mustard Sauce

THIS is my restaurant's most successful appetizer. After 20 years, it is still the most selected item. To look at it, you would never guess how simple it would be for you to make it at home. If you follow my directions carefully, you cannot go wrong—I promise!

makes 4 servings

4 ounces cream cheese

4 ounces shrimp, cut into $1/4$-inch cubes

4 ounces sea scallops, cut into $1/4$-inch cubes

4 ounces salmon, cut into $1/4$-inch cubes

1 tablespoon chopped fresh tarragon

1 tablespoon chopped fresh chives

$1/4$ teaspoon salt

$1/4$ teaspoon freshly ground black pepper

6 phyllo pastry sheets

olive oil cooking spray

extra-virgin olive oil, for brushing

Champagne Mustard Sauce (recipe on page 248)

Preheat oven to 400°F.

In a large glass bowl, beat the cream cheese until soft and creamy. Add the chopped seafood, tarragon, chives, salt, and pepper. Refrigerate for at least 1 hour.

Pull out 3 sheets of pastry at a time, keeping the rest of the dough covered with a slightly dampened towel (to keep it from drying out). Place the 3 sheets in front of you and spray the top sheet with the olive oil cooking spray. Starting 2 inches from the edge of the short side of the first sheet, spoon half of the seafood mixture, approximately to the thickness of an Italian sausage. Begin rolling the dough slowly, away from you, making a tight roll. At the end, spray the second sheet and place the stuffed roll on the edge of this sheet and roll both sheets toward you. Continue the same procedure with the third sheet, rolling away from you again. You will have one roll of 3 pastry sheets.

Spray, stuff, and roll the second strudel. Set the strudels on a nonstick baking sheet. Brush the tops lightly with the olive oil. Bake for 7 to 10 minutes until the phyllo is a nice golden brown. Let cool for 20 minutes. Refrigerate without covering for 2 hours.

To serve, cut each strudel in half. Then cut each half in half again. Then cut each quarter in half, but at an angle. You will have 8 pieces per strudel. On a nonstick baking sheet, stand each cut section of strudel on end, and reheat for 5 minutes.

Serve 4 pieces on each plate with the Champagne Mustard Sauce on the side.

Stuffed Vidalia Onions Topped with Goat Cheese

THIS recipe is the perfect showcase for Vidalia onions, those sweet and wonderful onions that arrive in supermarkets in May.

makes 4 servings

- 4 medium Vidalia or other sweet onions
- 1 tablespoon extra-virgin olive oil
- $^1/_4$ cup diced onions
- 1 pound lean ground beef
- 2 tablespoons fresh minced garlic
- 1 tablespoon chopped fresh thyme leaves
- 1 tablespoon chopped fresh rosemary leaves
- 1$^3/_4$ pounds ripe tomatoes, peeled, seeded, and chopped, to make 2 cups
- salt & freshly ground black pepper to taste
- 4 ounces goat cheese, frozen

Preheat oven to 375°F.

Slice off the tops of the onions. Using a melon ball cutter, empty the insides of the onions, leaving a $^1/_4$-inch shell. Poach the onion shells in hot water for approximately 15 minutes. Place cut side down on paper towels to drain. Refrigerate until ready to stuff.

In a saucepan, heat the olive oil then add the diced onions and cook until transparent. Add the ground beef and cook until golden brown. Stir in the garlic, thyme, and rosemary. When fragrant (about 30 seconds), add the tomatoes. Simmer slowly for 20 to 25 minutes. Adjust the seasoning with salt and pepper. Cool the mixture for approximately 1 hour in the refrigerator.

Remove the onions from the refrigerator and stuff each one with the beef mixture.

Grate 1 ounce of goat cheese on the top of each stuffed onion. Bake for approximately 15 to 20 minutes until the onions are very tender and the cheese has melted.

Phyllo Pastry Pizza with Broccoli Pesto, Tomatoes & Goat Cheese

THIS is a fantastic pizza! Not only is it low in fat, but it is very easy to make. All you need is a pizza screen. If your grocery store does not carry them, a good gourmet shop or restaurant supply house should. You can use the Broccoli Pesto, or any other pesto, for that matter. Just be sure to coat the bottom of the pizza with it.

makes one 9-inch pizza

7 sheets phyllo pastry

olive oil cooking spray

4 teaspoons freshly grated Reggiano Parmesan cheese, divided

1 tablespoon Broccoli Pesto (recipe on page 250)

1 tomato, peeled, seeded, and chopped

6 imported black olives, such as Kalamata, chopped

4 large basil leaves cut chiffonade (thin ribbons)

2 ounces goat cheese, frozen (for easy grating)

Preheat oven to 450°F.

Cut the 7 sheets of phyllo into large circles using the pizza screen as a guide. You can cut all the sheets at the same time. Spray the screen with olive oil cooking spray. Place the first sheet of phyllo on the screen, spray again lightly, and sprinkle on approximately $1/2$ teaspoon of the Parmesan cheese. Place the second sheet on top and repeat the same procedure with the spray and the cheese until you have placed the seventh sheet. Spread the Broccoli Pesto on top, arrange the tomatoes and the basil, and grate frozen goat cheese over top.

Bake in the oven for 3 to 5 minutes. Serve immediately.

59   incredible cuisine

Shrimp Roulade with Tequila-Lime Relish

THIS recipe is probably the most involved, so I've carefully pointed out the steps to guide you through. Believe me; it's worth it!

makes 4 servings

1 teaspoon chopped fresh parsley

1 teaspoon chopped fresh thyme

1 teaspoon chopped fresh chives

$1/2$ cup cream cheese, softened

1 cup fresh spinach leaves, washed and blanched

8 shrimp (15 count or larger), peeled and deveined

$1/2$ cup cornstarch

1 red bell pepper (roasted with the skin, seeds, and ribs removed, sliced julienne)

2 tablespoons flour seasoned with salt & freshly ground black pepper

2 egg whites, beaten until frothy

1 cup fresh white bread crumbs

2 tablespoons extra-virgin olive oil

Blend the fresh herbs into the cheese.

Blanch the spinach leaves for 2 minutes in boiling water and let cool.

Butterfly the shrimp (split them down the center, cutting almost but not completely through) and open them flat to resemble a butterfly shape. Dip the shrimp in cornstarch until completely covered. Place the shrimp between 2 sheets of plastic wrap and pound the shrimp to a $1/16$-inch thickness (picture 1). Place 1 spinach leaf on each shrimp. Pipe a 2-inch strip of cream cheese from head to tail down the center of the spinach (picture 2). Arrange a strip of bell pepper along one side of the cream cheese. Roll the flattened shrimp and refrigerate (picture 3).

A few minutes before serving time, dredge the shrimp rolls lightly in the seasoned flour, then in the egg whites, and then in the bread crumbs (picture 4).

Preheat oven to 350°F. In a nonstick ovenproof frying pan, heat the olive oil until hot. Brown the breaded shrimp rolls until golden brown (picture 5). Transfer the pan to the oven and bake for 8 to 10 minutes. Slice on the diagonal. Serve with the Tequila-Lime Relish.

tequila-lime relish

2 limes, peeled and cut into sections

2 ounces tequila, preferably Cuervo Gold

1 small white onion, diced

2 tablespoons hot pepper jelly

2 tablespoons white wine

1 tablespoon sherry or champagne vinegar

1 tablespoon fresh cilantro, chopped

1 teaspoon toasted cumin seeds

Mix all the ingredients and let stand for 1 hour. For garnish, use carrot peels and chives.

Sea Scallops in a Lime, Caper & Thyme Sauce

makes 4 servings

- 1 tablespoon extra-virgin olive oil
- ³/₄ pound sea scallops (20 to 30 count)
- 2 tablespoons minced shallots
- ¹/₄ cup Chardonnay or other full-bodied, dry white wine
- ¹/₄ cup evaporated skim milk
- 2 tablespoons small capers
- 1 lime, cut into segments
- 1 tablespoon fresh minced thyme leaves
- 4 scallop shells for serving
- thyme sprigs for garnish
- sea salt

In a sauté pan, heat the olive oil, add the scallops, and cook for 2 to 3 minutes on one side. Turn them on the other side, add the shallots, and cook for 2 minutes. Add the wine, evaporated milk, capers, lime segments, and thyme. Cook for 2 minutes.

Fill each scallop shell with the scallop mixture and decorate with thyme sprigs. Arrange sea salt on a serving plate. Place the filled shells on the sea salt and serve.

soups

Soup seems to be such an unappreciated—or maybe overlooked—food these days, and I can't understand why. Is there anyone who is not comforted on a cold winter night by a bowl of steaming, homemade soup?

And for a busy person, soup is absolutely the perfect food. It's easy to prepare, and you can even make it ahead; in fact, you should. Most soups taste better the next day. It's also versatile. Although many people don't think of it in this way, you can serve soup in cold or hot weather. In the winter, try my Roasted Corn Chowder (page 73) for a great lunch after a morning of sledding. In the summer, when the days are so hot you can't even think about cooking, have the Chilled Orange-Cucumber Soup (page 78); it's refreshing, elegant, and low-fat on top of it all!

But if you prepare only one recipe from this chapter, make it the Butternut Squash & Bourbon Bisque (page 70). It has very unusual ingredients, but the flavors marry so well! It's really an unbelievable taste sensation, and I know you're going to just love it.

Cream of Sweet Potato Soup

AS you will soon discover, my cream soups don't have cream! In this extremely simple recipe, the sweet potato provides plenty of texture, but more than half the flavor comes from the Chicken Stock. Feel free to substitute regular white potatoes, if you want. One last thing: Don't let the milk boil, or it will separate; if that happens, mix it again with an immersion blender.

makes 8 servings

1 tablespoon extra-virgin olive oil

$^1/_2$ cup chopped white onions

1 cup chopped leeks

1 cup chopped celery

2 large sweet potatoes, peeled and diced

3 tablespoons chopped fresh garlic

6 cups Chicken Stock (recipe on page 240)

1 tablespoon chopped fresh sage

$^1/_2$ cup evaporated skim milk

salt & freshly ground black pepper to taste

In a large soup kettle, heat the olive oil and add the onions. When onions become translucent, stir in the leeks and celery. Sweat the vegetables for 2 minutes. Add the sweet potatoes and garlic. When the garlic is fragrant, add the stock and sage. Cook for 25 minutes.

When the potatoes are tender, use an immersion blender to purée all vegetables until smooth. Add the evaporated milk and cook for 2 more minutes only. Do not bring to a boil.

Adjust seasonings and serve.

Vine-Ripened Tomato Soup

WAIT until you taste this soup! It is fantastic and so easy to prepare. But it is crucial that you use fresh ingredients—great, vine-ripened tomatoes that actually smell like tomatoes, and fresh thyme and basil.

makes 6 servings

- 1 tablespoon extra-virgin olive oil
- 1 leek, sliced into $1/2$-inch pieces
- 1 onion, diced
- 2 tablespoons chopped garlic
- 4 to 5 pounds vine-ripened tomatoes, cut into chunks OR two 28-ounce cans recipe-ready tomatoes
- 2 celery stalks, diced
- 5 cups Chicken Stock (recipe on page 240)
- $1/4$ cup tightly packed fresh basil leaves, chopped
- 1 tablespoon fresh thyme leaves
- kosher salt & freshly ground black pepper to taste
- garlic croutons, for garnish
- snipped chives, for garnish

Heat the olive oil in a large stockpot. Add the leeks and onions. When onions are translucent, stir in the garlic. When fragrant, add the tomatoes and celery. Add the stock, basil, and thyme.

Simmer for 30 to 40 minutes. Adjust the seasoning with salt and pepper.

Insert an immersion blender or pour the soup into a regular blender. Process until very smooth.

Serve with garlic croutons and a sprinkle of chives on top.

Cream of Wild Mushroom Soup with Couscous

WHEN I first demonstrated this recipe in my cooking school, I never heard so much noise with spoons hitting the plates—everyone was trying to get the last drop. This soup has a subtle Asian flavor that is absolutely outstanding, and it is very, very simple to make.

makes 6 servings

- 1 tablespoon extra-virgin olive oil
- 1 cup finely diced leeks
- 1 cup very finely diced onions
- 1 tablespoon chopped fresh garlic
- 1 teaspoon minced fresh ginger
- $1/2$ pound mixed wild mushrooms, chopped (cremini, shiitake, and oyster)—save 6 for decoration
- 2 tablespoons soy sauce
- 4 cups Roasted Chicken Stock (recipe on page 239)
- 1 cup port wine
- $1/2$ cup evaporated skim milk
- 3 tablespoons cornstarch mixed with 3 tablespoons water
- salt & freshly ground black pepper to taste
- 2 cups cooked couscous (recipe below)
- 6 chives, snipped, for garnish

In a large soup kettle, heat the olive oil and when hot, add the leeks and onions. When onions are golden brown, add the garlic and ginger. When garlic is fragrant, add the mushrooms and soy sauce. Sweat them for 2 minutes, then add the stock and port. Bring to a boil and simmer for 25 minutes. Pour in the evaporated milk and cornstarch mixture and heat for only 2 to 3 minutes; do not bring to a boil. Adjust seasonings.

In each soup plate, place $1/4$ cup cooked couscous. Pour about 1 cup of soup in the plate. Garnish with snipped chives and 1 or 2 very thinly sliced mushrooms.

couscous (optional)

- $2/3$ cup water
- 1 tablespoon extra-virgin olive oil
- salt to taste
- $1/2$ cup couscous (or you may substitute with regular pasta, rice, or orzo)

In a saucepan, bring the water, oil, and salt to a rolling boil. Add the couscous and immediately take it off the heat. Stir and let sit for 5 minutes. Fluff it with a fork and serve. Or, if used later, reheat in a microwave oven.

Butternut Squash & Bourbon Bisque

THIS has to be it—the finest soup I ever created in my life! The ingredients marry beautifully and create an unbelievable taste sensation.

makes 6 servings

1 or 2 butternut squash (about 4 pounds total)

1 tablespoon extra-virgin olive oil

1 cup diced onions

1 cup diced leeks

$1/2$ teaspoon ground cumin

2 tablespoons chopped fresh garlic

1 tablespoon chopped fresh ginger

2 tablespoons pure maple syrup

2 tablespoons soy sauce

$1/4$ cup bourbon

$1/2$ cup dry sherry

$1/4$ teaspoon grated nutmeg

5 cups Roasted Chicken Stock (recipe on page 239)

$3/4$ cup evaporated skim milk

salt & freshly ground black pepper to taste

2 tablespoons cornstarch mixed with 2 tablespoons water

Preheat oven to 375°F.

With a sharp knife, prick the squash in several places to allow steam to escape while it cooks (otherwise, it could burst). Place the squash in a baking dish lined with foil and roast for about 90 minutes, until the squash is soft when you push on it. Let cool for 30 minutes, so it's easier to handle, then peel, seed, and remove strings. Cut the roasted squash into $1/2$-inch pieces, or scoop meat out with a spoon.

In a heavy soup kettle, heat the olive oil and add the onions. Cook until light golden brown and add the leeks and cumin. Cook for 2 minutes and add the garlic and ginger. When the garlic is fragrant, add the maple syrup, soy sauce, bourbon, sherry, and nutmeg. Add the squash and stock and bring to a boil. Lower the heat and cook gently for 15 minutes.

Using an immersion blender (or a regular blender), purée the soup until very smooth. Add the evaporated milk, salt, and pepper. Cook for 2 minutes; do not bring to a boil. Add the cornstarch mixture and serve in soup plates.

If you like, garnish this soup with garlic and Parmesan cheese croutons and a dollop of nonfat sour cream.

Hearty Minestrone

ANOTHER quick and easy recipe. This is a terrific minestrone. Feel free to experiment a little with this one, definitely add more vegetables, if you have them on hand. Also, if you have some pesto in your freezer (as you should), go ahead and add a couple of big tablespoonfuls—it's fabulous!

makes 6 servings

1 tablespoon extra-virgin olive oil

1 cup chopped onions

1 cup chopped leeks (white part only)

5 cups Chicken Stock (recipe on page 240)

1 1/2 cups diced potatoes

1 cup orzo or small tube pasta

1 3/4 pounds ripe tomatoes, peeled, seeded, and chopped, to make 2 cups

1 cup white beans, cooked al dente

1 cup chopped yellow squash

1 cup chopped zucchini

2 cups stemmed spinach leaves

salt & freshly ground black pepper to taste

1/4 cup freshly grated Reggiano Parmesan cheese

In a soup kettle, heat the olive oil then add the onions. Sweat them for 2 minutes and add the leeks. Cook for 3 minutes. Add the stock and potatoes. Bring to a boil and reduce heat immediately to a slow simmer. Cook for 5 minutes. Add the orzo or tube pasta and cook for 5 additional minutes. Add the tomatoes, beans, squash, and zucchini. Cover and cook until vegetables are tender. Stir in the spinach and cook for 3 minutes. Adjust seasonings.

To serve, ladle into bowls and sprinkle with the Parmesan cheese.

Spicy Pinto Bean Soup

THE creamy, rich texture of this soup is created by blending half the cooked beans with the Chicken Stock, while leaving the rest whole. The cumin, allspice, and chili powder give this soup its unique flavor. I love to top it with a few croutons of freshly cut French bread.

makes 6 servings

- 1 tablespoon extra-virgin olive oil
- 3 ounces 97% fat-free smoked ham, cut into small dice
- 1 yellow onion, finely diced
- 1¹/₂ red bell peppers, finely diced
- ¹/₄ cup chopped fresh garlic
- 1 tablespoon chili powder
- 1 tablespoon ground cumin
- 1 teaspoon dried oregano
- ¹/₂ teaspoon ground allspice
- ¹/₄ teaspoon red pepper flakes
- 4 cups Chicken Stock (recipe on page 240)
- ¹/₂ cup dry sherry
- 2 bay leaves

In a large pot, heat the olive oil. Add the ham and cook until it begins to brown. Add the onions and sauté for 2 minutes, making sure the ham does not stick to the pot. Add the peppers and sauté for 2 minutes until they soften slightly. Add the garlic and, when fragrant, add all the spices and sauté for 1 minute. Add the stock, sherry, and bay leaves and bring to a boil. Simmer for 20 minutes. Remove bay leaves, add the reserved beans, and serve.

the beans

- 8 ounces dry pinto beans
- water to cover beans
- 3 cups Chicken Stock (recipe on page 240)
- salt to taste

Soak the beans overnight in just enough water to cover them. The next day, drain the beans, place in a small pot, cover with the stock, and bring to a boil. Simmer until beans are tender. Remove ¹/₂ of the beans from the pot and reserve. With an immersion blender, purée the remainder of the beans. Add salt to taste. Add the reserved whole beans back into the pot and set aside.

Roasted Corn Chowder

I could eat the entire pot of this soup! Your guests will feel the same way—it is outstanding. And you do not have to roast the corn yourself; you can buy frozen corn, already cooked.

makes 8 servings

6 cups Chicken Stock (recipe on page 240)

2 pounds potatoes, peeled and diced

1 tablespoon extra-virgin olive oil

$^{1}/_{4}$ cup diced 97% fat-free smoked ham

$^{1}/_{2}$ cup diced onions

$^{1}/_{2}$ cup diced leeks

$^{1}/_{2}$ cup diced celery

$^{1}/_{2}$ red bell pepper, cut into brunoise (tiny dice)

$^{1}/_{2}$ green bell pepper, cut into brunoise (tiny dice)

1 tablespoon chopped fresh thyme leaves

salt & freshly ground black pepper to taste

1 tablespoon evaporated skim milk

2 tablespoons cornstarch mixed with 2 tablespoons water

roasted corn

2 ears corn, in husks

In a large soup kettle, heat the stock. Add the potatoes and cook until tender. In the meantime, roast the corn in the oven (see instructions below). When potatoes are tender, use an immersion blender and purée until very smooth.

In another soup kettle, heat the olive oil and when hot, add the ham and onions. When the onions are translucent, add the leeks, celery, bell peppers, and thyme. Sweat them for 5 minutes. Add the puréed potatoes to the vegetables. Mix in the roasted corn kernels, adjust seasonings, and cook for 5 more minutes.

Add the evaporated milk, bring to a boil, and add the cornstarch mixture. Cook for 2 more minutes only; do not bring to a boil. Serve immediately.

Preheat oven to 425°F.

Remove the outer layers of husks, except for two. Expose the kernels and rub them with a very light coating of olive oil, salt, and pepper. Replace the two layers of husks and place on a baking sheet. Bake for 30 minutes. Remove the kernels from the corn husks for the corn chowder.

Corn & Shrimp Bisque

YOU'LL notice that the first step of this recipe is to purée a third of the corn and the stock, along with the cilantro; this is what will provide the texture in this fabulous soup. Sweating the onions and peppers will make them sweeter and also add some moisture. And the evaporated milk is what makes it a bisque. Few of my recipes are easier or quicker than this one!

makes 6 servings

3 cups frozen or fresh corn kernels, divided

3 cups Chicken Stock (recipe on page 240), divided

1/4 cup chopped fresh cilantro

1 tablespoon extra-virgin olive oil

1/2 cup chopped onions

1/2 cup diced red bell peppers

1/2 cup diced green bell peppers

salt & freshly ground black pepper to taste

1 tablespoon chopped fresh thyme leaves

1/2 pound baby shrimp (60 to 70 count), peeled and deveined

1/2 cup evaporated skim milk

In a blender, combine 1 cup of the corn, 1 cup of the stock, and the cilantro. Blend until very smooth.

In a soup kettle over medium heat, heat the olive oil, then add the onions, peppers, salt, pepper, and thyme. Cook for 3 minutes. Add the blended corn mixture and the remaining 2 cups stock and 2 cups corn kernels. Bring to a slow boil, then add the shrimp. Cover and cook for 5 minutes. Add the evaporated milk and adjust seasonings, if necessary.

Creamy Shiitake Mushroom & Barley Soup

THIS is a marvelous mushroom and barley soup. I suggest using the shiitake mushrooms, but you should feel free to substitute cremini or even the regular variety; they would certainly work just as well. Be careful as you add the cornstarch at the end. Add it gradually, and see what happens; you don't want it to get too thick.

makes 6 servings

1 tablespoon extra-virgin olive oil

1 cup chopped onions

2 scallions, sliced into $^{1}/_{4}$-inch pieces

2 tablespoons chopped fresh garlic

$^{1}/_{2}$ cup barley

2 cups chopped shiitake mushrooms, sliced

4 cups beef broth

2 tablespoons dry vermouth

salt & freshly ground black pepper to taste

$^{1}/_{2}$ cup evaporated skim milk

2 tablespoons cornstarch mixed with 2 tablespoons water

In a large soup kettle, heat the olive oil then add the onions. Sweat them for 5 minutes until light golden brown and add the scallions. Cook for 2 minutes and add the garlic. When the garlic becomes fragrant, add the barley and mushrooms. Mix well and add the beef broth and vermouth. Season with salt and pepper and let simmer for 30 minutes. Add the evaporated milk and the cornstarch mixture. Adjust seasonings, if necessary.

Mediterranean Clam Chowder with Almond Pesto

IT is called "Mediterranean" because it has fennel, garlic, thyme, oregano, tomato, and pesto—the signature ingredients of Mediterranean cooking. The herbs give it some punch, but the main flavor comes from the Almond Pesto, which is what really finishes the soup off and gives it a wonderful personality. Use mussels instead of clams, if you want; the chowder will still taste splendid.

makes 6 servings

1 tablespoon extra-virgin olive oil

6 ounces 97% fat-free smoked ham, cut into $^1/_4$-inch cubes

1 cup diced onions

1 cup diced leeks

2 cups diced potatoes ($^3/_4$ inch)

1 cup diced carrots

1 cup diced celery

1 cup diced fresh fennel

2 tablespoons chopped fresh garlic

1 tablespoon chopped fresh thyme leaves

1 tablespoon chopped fresh oregano

6 cups Chicken Stock (recipe on page 240)

1$^3/_4$ pounds ripe tomatoes, peeled, seeded, and dried, to make 2 cups

4 dozen clams, approximately

4 tablespoons Almond Pesto (recipe on page 249)

salt & freshly ground black pepper to taste

In a soup kettle, heat the olive oil then add the ham and onions. Cook until the onions are translucent. Add the leeks and sweat them for 2 more minutes. Add the potatoes, carrots, celery, and fennel. Add the garlic and when fragrant, add the thyme and oregano. Pour in the stock and cook for approximately 30 minutes.

While the stock is simmering, place the clams in a large pot, add $^1/_2$ cup water, and cover tightly. Steam over high heat for 5 to 7 minutes and transfer the opened clams to a bowl. Discard any clams that do not open. Remove about half of the clams from the shells and set aside. (The clams in their shells will be used to garnish the soup before serving.)

Add the tomatoes to the soup and simmer for 15 more minutes. Stir in the shucked clams, Almond Pesto, salt, and pepper to taste.

Ladle the soup into bowls and garnish with the clams in their shells.

Chilled Orange-Cucumber Soup

COLD soups are so uncommon—but they are so delicious! And, they're perfect on a hot summer day. I can never have enough.

makes 4 servings

1 tablespoon extra-virgin olive oil

1/2 cup diced white onions

1/2 cup diced leeks (white part only)

3 cups peeled and cubed European cucumbers, divided

1/2 cup orange juice concentrate

2 cups Chicken Stock (recipe on page 240)

1 cup low-fat yogurt

1/2 cup low-fat sour cream

1 tablespoon grated orange zest

salt & freshly ground black pepper to taste

cilantro leaves for garnish

In a large, nonstick saucepan, heat the olive oil and add the onions and leeks. Cook for 3 to 4 minutes until translucent. Add 2 cups of the cucumber cubes, the orange juice concentrate, and the stock. Cook for 15 minutes.

Insert an immersion blender or transfer the mixture to a blender or food processor and blend until very smooth. Allow the mixture to cool in the refrigerator for a minimum of 2 hours. Then add the yogurt, sour cream, orange zest, salt and pepper, and the remaining 1 cup cucumber cubes. Chill the mixture and serve in chilled bowls. Garnish with cilantro leaves

Cold Beet Soup with Sour Cream

makes 4 servings

4 medium beets

4 whole cloves

1 bay leaf

3/4 cup sour cream

1/4 cup vodka

1 ripe tomato, quartered

1 tablespoon chopped fresh ginger

1/4 teaspoon Tabasco sauce

1/2 cup low-fat yogurt

salt & freshly ground black pepper to taste

chives, sour cream, and croutons for garnish

Scrub the beets. When you cut off the stems, leave at least 1 inch; this prevents the beet from leaking into the water. Put the beet juice in a pot of water along with the cloves and bay leaf. Boil for at least 1 hour, or until the beets are tender and cooked all the way through. Transfer immediately to ice water.

Peel the beets and cut into cubes. Transfer to a blender or food processor. Add the sour cream, vodka, tomato, ginger, and Tabasco. Blend until very smooth. To improve the texture, press the mixture through a fine sieve.

Add the yogurt and salt and pepper. Refrigerate for at least 4 hours. Ladle into ice-cold bowls and garnish with chives, sour cream, and croutons.

pasta & rice

Although I grew up in France, my mother is actually from Italy; so you can be sure we would eat pasta at least a few times a week in our house. To this day, I still love pasta, and still eat it as often as I did as a boy! If you love it as much as I do, double the batch when you're making the sauce for a recipe, and freeze the rest to use later to pour over a bunch of spaghetti or fettuccine.

Risotto was another staple in our house, and now it's one of the things I most enjoy making when I want a delicious, comforting meal, and I have the time to enjoy it. Risotto just cannot be rushed. It takes time for the Arborio rice to slowly release its starch and become creamy—28 minutes, to be exact. Many people don't appreciate this, and add the meat or vegetable stock too quickly. But once risotto is ready, it's ready, and you must be prepared to serve it immediately. "Risotto waits for no one," my mother used to say. To me, it's perfect for a Friday night supper or a casual meal with a few friends; everyone can relax in the kitchen with a glass of wine, chatting as you stir, stir, stir.

Angel Hair Pasta with Chicken Tenderloin, Broccoli & Mascarpone Cheese

BE careful when you add the nutmeg to this sauce; you don't want too much! And be sure to plunge the broccoli in ice water after you blanch it, to seal in that beautiful green color.

makes 4 servings

1 pound angel hair pasta (cappellini)

1 bunch broccoli (florets only)

1 tablespoon extra-virgin olive oil

1 pound chicken tenderloins

$1/2$ cup pearl onions

4 ounces 97% fat-free smoked ham, cut into $1/4$-inch cubes

1 cup Chicken Stock (recipe on page 240)

2 tablespoons tomato purée

$1/2$ teaspoon grated nutmeg

8 ounces mascarpone cheese

$1/2$ cup freshly grated Reggiano Parmesan cheese

2 tablespoons chopped fresh cilantro

salt & freshly ground black pepper to taste

Cook the pasta according to package directions.

Blanch the broccoli florets in boiling, salted water until tender but not overcooked.

In a Dutch oven, heat the olive oil, then add the chicken tenderloins and pearl onions. Cook until chicken pieces are golden brown on both sides. Add the ham, stock, tomato purée, and nutmeg. Cook for 5 minutes. Add the mascarpone, Parmesan, and cilantro. Cook for 30 seconds: No more, or the mascarpone will separate. Add the blanched broccoli. Adjust the seasoning with salt and pepper.

Add the cooked pasta to the pot, mix well, and serve immediately.

Saffron Fettuccine with Shellfish & Almond Pesto Sauce

THE pesto is the signature ingredient in this very flavorful recipe. The Kalamata olives and the Pernod give it a Mediterranean feeling.

1 tablespoon extra-virgin olive oil

3/4 pound medium-large shrimp (21 to 25 count), peeled and deveined

3/4 pound sea scallops (20 to 30 count)

1 tablespoon chopped fresh garlic

1 pound ripe tomatoes, peeled, seeded, and chopped, to make 1 cup

2 tablespoons sherry

3/4 cup Chicken Stock (recipe on page 240)

1/4 cup chopped imported black Kalamata olives

2 tablespoons Almond Pesto (recipe on page 249)

1 teaspoon Pernod liqueur

24 mussels, scrubbed

1 pound saffron fettuccine or other fresh pasta

In a sauté pan, heat the olive oil. Add the shrimp and cook on both sides for 2 minutes. Add the scallops and sauté for 1 minute on each side. Add the garlic and when fragrant, add the tomatoes and sherry. Stir in the stock, olives, Almond Pesto, Pernod, and mussels. Cover and cook for 2 more minutes, or until the mussels open.

In the meantime, cook the fettuccine according to package directions. Drain and divide the pasta among 6 dinner plates. Spoon the seafood and the sauce over the pasta. Serve immediately.

Low-Fat Two-Sauce Lasagna

I was raised on lasagna and, let me tell you, this is the finest recipe I've ever tasted! I make this often in cooking class and no one can ever tell it's low-fat.

makes 8 servings

15 lasagna noodles

2 cups Low-Fat Béchamel Sauce (recipe below)

two 8-ounce boneless, skinless chicken breasts, sautéed on all sides and thinly sliced

10 thin slices 97% fat-free baked ham, cut into approximately 1-inch squares

2 cups Turkey Bolognese Sauce (recipe on facing page)

3/4 cup freshly grated Reggiano Parmesan cheese and 3/4 cup freshly grated provolone cheese, mixed together

Preheat oven to 375°F. Coat a 13-inch x 9-inch baking dish with an olive oil cooking spray.

Cook the noodles in boiling water until barely cooked and beginning to soften—no more than 3 minutes. Spread them on a kitchen towel to absorb the moisture.

Cover the bottom of the baking dish with a layer of noodles and spread half of the Béchamel Sauce over the pasta. Sprinkle with half of the chicken and ham slices, 1/4 of the Parmesan-and-provolone mixture and cover with a second layer of pasta. Spread half of the Turkey Bolognese Sauce and 1/4 of the cheese mixture. Cover with a third layer of the pasta. Spread the remaining half of the Béchamel and the chicken and ham. Sprinkle 1/4 of the cheese mixture and cover with the last layer of the pasta. Spread the remaining half of the Bolognese Sauce and top with the last of the cheese.

Cover and bake for 1 hour. Let it rest for 10 minutes before serving.

low-fat béchamel sauce

2 tablespoons sunflower oil

1/4 cup all-purpose flour

3 cups low-fat milk, divided

1/2 teaspoon grated nutmeg

salt & freshly ground black pepper to taste

In a saucepan, heat the oil and, over low heat, add the flour. With a wooden spoon, cook while mixing continuously, until the flour turns a very light brown. (It should take no more than 3 minutes and remain a very light hazelnut-brown color.)

In a separate pan, scald the milk. Add 1 1/2 cups of the milk to the flour and whisk continuously, until the sauce starts to bubble and thicken. Simmer for 2 to 3 minutes, stirring continuously with a wooden spoon. Thin out the sauce as necessary with the remaining 1 1/2 cups milk. The sauce should be thick enough to coat the back of a spoon. Season with the nutmeg, salt, and pepper. If there are lumps, strain the sauce through a fine sieve.

turkey bolognese sauce

1 tablespoon extra-virgin olive oil

1 cup diced yellow onions

1 pound lean turkey meat, ground

$^1/_4$ pound button mushrooms, quartered

2 tablespoons chopped garlic

$4^1/_2$ pounds ripe tomatoes, peeled, seeded, and diced, to make 5 cups OR two 28-ounce cans recipe-ready tomatoes

2 tablespoons tomato paste

1 teaspoon fresh thyme leaves, chopped

1 teaspoon fresh oregano leaves, chopped

$^1/_4$ cup Chicken Stock, if necessary (recipe on page 240)

salt & freshly ground black pepper to taste

In a large soup kettle or Dutch oven, heat the olive oil over medium heat. Add the onions and sauté for 2 minutes. Add the ground turkey and cook until nice and golden brown. Add the mushrooms and garlic and sauté for 2 minutes. When the garlic becomes fragrant, add the tomatoes, tomato paste, thyme, and oregano. Simmer slowly for 30 minutes, adding a little stock if the sauce becomes too thick. Adjust the seasoning with salt and pepper.

Fresh Linguine with Mussels & Shrimp in a Pernod Sauce

THIS is good to do when you have a bunch of friends in the kitchen. Have each person chop something up, and the ingredients will be ready in no time—and you'll all have fun in the process!

makes 6 servings

2 tablespoons extra-virgin olive oil, divided

1 1/2 pounds mussels, scrubbed

1/2 cup Chardonnay or other full-bodied, dry white wine

2 tablespoons chopped fresh cilantro

2 shallots, chopped

1/2 red bell pepper, julienne

1/2 green bell pepper, julienne

1/2 yellow bell pepper, julienne

1/4 Scotch bonnet pepper, finely chopped

1 pound baby shrimp (60 to 70 count)

1 tablespoon grated orange zest

1 tablespoon chopped fresh thyme leaves

1 cup Chicken Stock (recipe on page 240)

1/2 cup evaporated milk

2 tablespoons cornstarch mixed with 2 tablespoons water

1 tablespoon Pernod liqueur

2 tablespoons chopped fresh parsley

salt & freshly ground black pepper to taste

1 pound fresh linguine

In a large saucepan or soup kettle, heat 1 tablespoon olive oil, then add the mussels, wine, and cilantro. Cover and cook 3 to 4 minutes. Transfer the opened mussels to a glass bowl to cool. Discard any mussels that have not opened. Detach and discard the top halves of the shells. Set the mussels aside in a warm place.

Place another saucepan on medium heat and heat the remaining 1 tablespoon olive oil. When hot, add the shallots and sweat for 1 minute. Add the bell peppers and Scotch bonnet pepper. Cook until the peppers are fragrant and tender. Add the shrimp and cook for 2 minutes. Add the orange zest and thyme. Pour in the stock and the evaporated milk, and when hot, add the cornstarch mixture. Stir in the Pernod and parsley. Adjust the seasoning with salt and pepper.

In the meantime, cook the linguine according to package directions. Divide the linguine into 6 soup plates. Pour the sauce on top of the pasta. Arrange the mussels around the edge of each plate. Sprinkle with parsley for a final touch.

Fresh Egg Fettuccine with Chicken & Wild Mushrooms

THE first time I prepared this phenomenal dish was on the Today Show. I received over 22,000 recipe requests, and I still get them! Now you, too, can try it at home. It's very, very simple. The key is to use evaporated milk, which you should always have in your pantry, and a good-quality fettuccine. Feel free to substitute regular mushrooms for the more exotic ones. But be careful to add the dissolved cornstarch slowly, a bit at a time.

makes 6 servings

1 tablespoon extra-virgin olive oil

1 pound chicken tenderloins OR 3 skinless breasts, cut into $1/2$-inch strips

$1/4$ pound 97% fat-free smoked ham, cut into $1/4$-inch strips

$1/4$ pound mixed wild mushrooms (cremini, oyster, and shiitake)

3 scallions, cut on the diagonal into $1/2$-inch-wide strips

$3/4$ cup evaporated milk

$3/4$ cup Chicken Stock (recipe on page 240)

$1/4$ cup freshly grated Reggiano Parmesan cheese

$1/4$ teaspoon grated nutmeg

1 tablespoon cornstarch mixed with 2 tablespoons water

$3/4$ pound fresh egg fettuccine

1 tablespoon snipped fresh chives, for garnish

In a large sauté pan, heat the olive oil and add the chicken pieces. Cook until a golden color on each side. Add the ham, mushrooms, and scallions. Cook for about 5 minutes, then add the evaporated milk, stock, Parmesan cheese, nutmeg, and the dissolved cornstarch mixture. Remove from heat as soon as it comes to a boil.

In the meantime, cook the fettuccine according to package directions. Drain and combine the pasta with the chicken and mushroom mixture. Mix very well so that all the noodles are well coated.

Divide equally onto serving plates. Sprinkle with chives. Serve immediately.

Rigatoni with Pine Nuts, Sun-Dried Tomatoes & Goat Cheese

I discovered yellow banana peppers by accident. I saw them in a jar at the grocery store and thought they looked beautiful, and I've used them a lot ever since. They're an interesting pepper—sweet and somewhat bitter at the same time. If you have trouble finding them, substitute regular bell peppers.

makes 4 servings

1 tablespoon extra-virgin olive oil

1/2 red onion, cut into very thin slices

4 yellow banana peppers, diced 1/4 inch

1/3 cup sliced imported black olives, such as Kalamata

2 tablespoons sun-dried tomatoes

1/2 cup roasted pine nuts, toasted

1 cup Chicken Stock (recipe on page 240)

1 pound rigatoni, cooked according to package directions

4 ounces goat cheese

salt & freshly ground black pepper to taste

In a sauté pan, heat the olive oil and sweat the onions until translucent. Add the banana peppers, olives, sun-dried tomatoes, pine nuts, and the stock. Bring to a boil. Add the cooked pasta and the goat cheese. Mix for 2 minutes, just long enough to melt the cheese. Adjust the seasoning with salt and pepper.

Serve immediately.

Parmesan & Potato Gnocchi

RESIST the temptation to add egg yolk—you don't need it, you just don't need it. This recipe will produce a light, not gummy, gnocchi. And be sure to use Idaho potatoes.

makes 6 servings

2 pounds Idaho baking potatoes

$^3/_4$ teaspoon salt, divided

1 tablespoon chopped fresh sage

$1^1/_4$ cups all-purpose flour

$^1/_2$ cup grated Reggiano Parmesan cheese

Spiced Tomato & Basil Sauce (recipe on page 245)

Preheat oven to 400°F.

Bake the potatoes for 1 hour, or until tender. Let cool 5 minutes. Using a potholder to hold the hot potatoes, peel them with a paring knife. Using a ricer fitted with the smallest disk, rice the peeled potatoes. Add $^1/_2$ teaspoon of the salt and the sage. Allow approximately 10 minutes for the steam to subside.

Sprinkle the flour and cheese into the riced potatoes very slowly and gently. Using your hand, incorporate all the flour until the dough is very smooth.

Cut the dough into 4 or 5 balls. Roll each one into a long sausage-shaped roll. Cut the roll into pieces about $^3/_4$ to 1 inch in length.

Using the back of a floured fork, press ridges into one side of the gnocchi. Make an indentation on the other side. This will allow the gnocchi to cook evenly and will also create ridges to hold the sauce.

In a large soup kettle, heat at least 5 quarts of water. Add $^1/_4$ teaspoon salt and bring to a boil. Reduce to medium heat and poach the gnocchi, 2 dozen at a time, until they float. It should not take more than 2 minutes for each batch.

Retrieve the gnocchi from the water with a slotted spoon and transfer to a warm plate. Repeat until all gnocchi are cooked.

Serve with the Spiced Tomato & Basil Sauce.

Pasta!

Penne with Garlic-&-Cilantro Cream

THE key to the success of this incredible dish is the garlic: Roasted or poached, you are going to love it. Chicken tenderloin also works well instead of the baby shrimp.

makes 4 servings

1 whole garlic head

2 tablespoons extra-virgin olive oil, divided

2 shallots, minced

$1/4$ cup Chicken Stock (recipe on page 240)

$1/2$ cup evaporated skim milk

1 tablespoon cornstarch mixed with 1 tablespoon water

1 pound penne or other sturdy pasta

$1/2$ pound baby shrimp (60 to 70 count), peeled and deveined

salt & freshly ground black pepper to taste

2 tablespoons chopped fresh cilantro leaves

$1/2$ cup freshly grated Reggiano Parmesan cheese (optional)

* Roast the garlic or poach it. If you roast the garlic, it will have a nutty flavor.

In a saucepan, heat 1 tablespoon of the olive oil and add the shallots. When light golden brown, stir in the stock and roasted or poached garlic. Bring to a boil and add the evaporated milk and the cornstarch mixture. Transfer to a blender and blend thoroughly until very smooth. Strain through a fine sieve.

Cook the pasta according to package directions. In the meantime, in a sauté pan, heat the remaining 1 tablespoon olive oil and cook the baby shrimp on both sides. Add the creamy garlic mixture. Season with salt, pepper, and cilantro. Add the Parmesan cheese, if using, and mix well. Add the pasta and toss to coat well. Serve immediately.

* Roasting Method:

Preheat oven to 375°F. Do not remove the papery outer skin from the garlic. With a very sharp knife, cut the garlic head in half sideways. Set the garlic halves, cut side up, on a piece of foil, then drizzle each half with 1 tablespoon olive oil. Arrange sprigs of rosemary on each half and sprinkle with freshly ground black pepper. Close the foil and roast for about 45 minutes, or until tender and buttery. Let cool, then slip the cloves out of the skins.

* Poaching Method:

Separate the cloves of the head of garlic, but do not peel them. Bring two small saucepans of water to a boil, then put the garlic in one of them. Poach for 7 minutes, then drain and return the garlic to the other pot of boiling water. Let cook for 7 minutes, then drain and return garlic to the first pot, once again filled with boiling water, for final blanching. This will eliminate any bitterness. Cool the garlic briefly, then slip the cloves out of their skins.

Tabouli Provençale

THERE has not been a summer when we did not have tabouli in my house. I serve a big ice-cream scoopful with every sandwich and lunch I prepare. It is also excellent as a main salad on a buffet table. And it is the most simple pasta to make! I personally eat it with a big spoon and usually don't stop until the bowl is clean.

makes 8 servings

1¼ cups water

½ cup freshly squeezed lemon juice

2 tablespoons extra-virgin olive oil

½ teaspoon salt

1 garlic clove, chopped

1 cup couscous

In a saucepan, bring the water, lemon juice, olive oil, salt, and garlic to a rolling boil. Add the couscous and immediately take it off the heat. Stir and let sit for 5 minutes. Fluff with a fork, refrigerate for at least 2 hours.

the tabouli

1 pound cherry tomatoes, quartered

1¼ cups parsley leaves, chopped and dried

¼ cup mint leaves, chopped

½ red bell pepper, cut into brunoise (tiny dice)

½ green bell pepper, cut into brunoise

½ yellow pepper, cut into brunoise

¼ cup freshly squeezed lemon juice

salt & freshly ground black pepper to taste

1 tablespoon extra-virgin olive oil

1 tablespoon balsamic vinegar

Mix all the ingredients with the cooled couscous and serve cold.

Turkey & Herb Cheese Ravioli

THIS is not as complicated as it looks. The steps are quite simple. You can even skip making the ravioli and use your favorite noodles instead.

makes 4 servings
(2 ravioli per person)

1 tablespoon extra-virgin olive oil

$1/2$ cup finely minced onions

$1/4$ cup finely diced 97% fat-free smoked ham

salt & freshly ground black pepper to taste

$1/2$ pound lean ground turkey breast

$1/2$ cup minced celery

1 tablespoon minced garlic

1 tablespoon chopped fresh thyme leaves

1 pound ripe tomatoes, peeled, seeded, and chopped, to make 1 cup

2 tablespoons tomato purée

16 wonton skins (found in the produce section of large supermarkets)

4 egg whites, lightly beaten

Roasted Garlic & Tomato Sauce (recipe on page 247)

In a sauté pan, heat the olive oil, then add the onions, ham, salt, and pepper. Sweat them for 2 minutes. Add the crumbled ground turkey and cook until golden brown. Add the celery and garlic. When the garlic becomes fragrant, add the thyme, tomatoes, and tomato purée. Season with salt and pepper to taste. Cook for 20 minutes and let it cool for about 45 minutes. In a large glass bowl, mix the cheese mixture with the turkey mixture. (It is best to refrigerate the mixture for 2 hours so it will hold together very tightly.)

Place the 16 wonton skins on a clean work surface. Using a small paintbrush or your fingertips, "paint" the egg whites onto one side of each wonton skin. Place 1 tablespoon of the turkey and cheese mixture in the center of 8 of the squares. Place a second wonton skin on top of each filled bottom (painted side down) and press firmly to close.

Using a cookie cutter, a fluted cutter, or a knife, cut out $2^1/_2$-inch circles and discard the excess wonton skin. You may refrigerate the ravioli, covered, in a single layer on a baking sheet. Bring a potful of water to a boil. Cook the ravioli until they float to the top, 7 to 10 minutes. Serve with the Roasted Garlic & Tomato Sauce.

herb cream cheese

8 ounces low-fat cream cheese

1 tablespoon chopped fresh garlic

1 teaspoon chopped fresh thyme

1 teaspoon chopped fresh oregano leaves

$1/4$ teaspoon salt

$1/4$ teaspoon freshly ground black pepper

In a glass bowl, blend the cheese with all the ingredients and refrigerate.

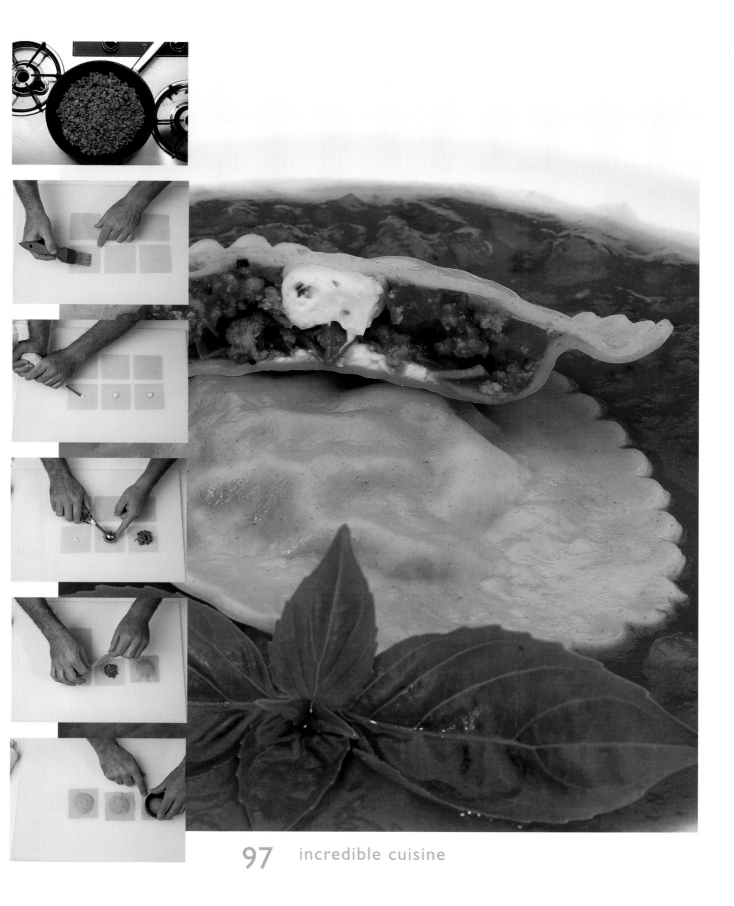

97   incredible cuisine

Chicken, Mushroom & Mascarpone Ravioli with Port Wine & Pine Nut Sauce

**makes 4 servings
(3 ravioli per person)**

1 tablespoon extra-virgin olive oil

2 tablespoons onions, diced

1 large boneless chicken breast, cut into $1/4$-inch cubes

$1/4$ pound button mushrooms, sliced

2 scallions, cut into $1/8$-inch slices

salt & freshly ground black pepper to taste

6 ounces mascarpone cheese

24 wonton skins, approximately 3 x 3 inches (found in the produce section of large supermarkets)

4 egg whites, lightly beaten

In a sauté pan, heat the olive oil, add the onions and cook until translucent. Add the chicken cubes and the mushrooms and cook until the chicken is golden brown. Add the scallions. Season with salt and pepper. Remove from the heat. Add the mascarpone cheese and mix. Transfer to a cold glass bowl and refrigerate for 2 hours.

Place the 24 wonton skins on a clean work surface. Using your fingertips, "paint" the egg whites onto one side of each wonton skin. Place 1 tablespoon of the chicken-and-cheese stuffing mixture in the center of 12 of the squares. Place a second wonton skin on top of each filled bottom (painted side down) and press firmly to close.

Using a cookie cutter, a fluted cutter, or a knife, cut $2^1/2$-inch circles and discard the excess wonton skin. You may refrigerate the ravioli, covered, in a single layer on a baking sheet. Bring a potful of water to a boil. Cook the ravioli until they float to the top, about 7 to 10 minutes.

port wine & pine nut sauce

1 tablespoon extra-virgin olive oil

2 shallots, minced

$1/4$ cup balsamic vinegar

3 tablespoons low-sodium soy sauce

$1/4$ cup port wine

$1/2$ cup Beef Stock (recipe on page 238)

1 tablespoon chopped fresh thyme leaves

1 tablespoon cornstarch mixed with 1 tablespoon water

salt & freshly ground black pepper to taste

$1/4$ cup toasted pine nuts* (reserve 2 tablespoons for garnish)

2 tablespoons chopped fresh cilantro (reserve 1 teaspoon for garnish)

In a saucepan, heat the olive oil and add the shallots. Cook until light golden brown. Be sure to mix them with a wooden spoon so that they do not burn. Add the balsamic vinegar and soy sauce and let reduce until 2 tablespoons remain. Add the port wine and let reduce by half. Add the stock and thyme. Let reduce for 5 minutes on high heat.

Add the cornstarch mixture and salt and pepper. Cook for 2 minutes. The sauce should be thick enough to coat the back of a spoon. If not, add a touch more of cornstarch diluted in water. Stir in the pine nuts and cilantro. Mix well.

To serve, spoon about 2 or 3 tablespoons of sauce onto the center of each plate. Arrange 3 ravioli per plate, sprinkle the remaining pine nuts and cilantro to garnish.

* Note on Pine Nuts: To toast pine nuts, simply put them in a preheated 400°F oven for about 5 minutes. They should turn a nice golden brown.

Zucchini, Yellow Squash & Cremini Risotto

I could write a book just on risotto. My mom used to make the finest risottos! Believe me, if you follow my exact instructions, you can, too. Be sure to use Italian Arborio rice (available in any good Italian market), and remember: Add the stock only 1 cup at a time.

makes 4 servings

6 cups (approximately) Chicken Stock (recipe on page 240)

3 tablespoons extra-virgin olive oil, divided

1 cup diced onions

2 cups Arborio rice (No substitutions!)

salt & freshly ground black pepper to taste

1 cup Chardonnay or other full-bodied, dry white wine

¹/₄ cup diced red bell pepper

1¹/₂ pounds sliced cremini mushrooms

1 cup diced zucchini

1 cup diced yellow squash

1 cup freshly grated Reggiano Parmesan cheese (optional)

Heat the stock in a saucepan.

In a heavy-bottom soup kettle (approximately 12 inches in diameter and 4 to 6 inches deep), heat 2 tablespoons of the olive oil. When hot, add the onions. When the onions become a light golden brown, add the rice, salt, and pepper. Toss the rice constantly until the grains turn light gold in color. Add the wine. When all the wine has been absorbed by the rice, add 1 cup of hot stock. Simmer very slowly until all the stock has been absorbed. Continue adding more stock, 1 cup at a time, allowing the stock to be absorbed completely between each addition.

In the meantime, in a sauté pan, heat the remaining 1 tablespoon olive oil. Add the bell peppers and sweat them for 2 minutes. Add the mushrooms, zucchini, and yellow squash. Cook for 2 minutes. Add 1 cup of stock, cover and let simmer for 5 to 7 minutes.

Return to the rice and add more stock until all has been absorbed. Continue to stir slowly. Add the vegetable mixture and continue to stir until almost all the liquid has been absorbed. Adjust the seasoning with salt and pepper, if needed, and stir in the Parmesan cheese, if using.

Serve immediately.

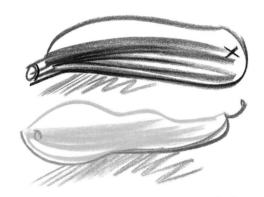

Sun-Dried Tomato, Basil &
Goat Cheese Risotto

THIS is a fantastic risotto recipe. I just love the combination of sun-dried tomatoes and goat cheese, but you may use a good blue cheese instead of the goat cheese, if you prefer. Be sure to add the stock 1 cup at a time, and wait for it to be absorbed before adding the next cup. This lets the rice cook from the inside out, rather than the outside in, and keeps it creamy, not sticky.

makes 4 servings

6 cups (approximately) Chicken Stock (recipe on page 240)

3 tablespoons extra-virgin olive oil, divided

1 cup diced onions

salt & freshly ground black pepper to taste

2 cups Arborio rice (No substitutions!)

1 cup Chardonnay or other full-bodied, dry white wine

1 cup reconstituted and chopped sun-dried tomatoes

$^1/_4$ cup chopped fresh basil

$^1/_2$ cup freshly grated Reggiano Parmesan cheese

$^1/_4$ cup goat cheese

Heat the stock in a saucepan.

In a heavy-bottom soup kettle (approximately 12 inches in diameter and 4 to 6 inches deep), heat 2 tablespoons of the olive oil and when hot, add the onions, salt, and pepper. When the onions become a light golden brown, add the rice. Toss the rice constantly until the grains turn light gold in color.

Add the wine and when all the wine has been absorbed by the rice, add 1 cup stock. When that has been absorbed, add a second cup of stock. After the second cup has been absorbed, mix in the sun-dried tomatoes and basil. Cook over medium to high heat until all the stock has been absorbed. Continue adding the stock, 1 cup at a time, allowing the stock to be absorbed completely between each addition.

Adjust the seasoning with salt and pepper, if needed. Stir in the Parmesan cheese and goat cheese and mix well for 1 minute. Serve immediately.

Shrimp & Scallion Risotto

TO prepare a great risotto, timing is most important. Make sure you have all your ingredients ready in advance. You can substitute the shrimp with lobster or sea scallops, if you desire. But you must serve this as soon as it's ready; as my mother used to say, risotto waits for no one!

makes 4 servings

6 cups (approximately) Chicken Stock (recipe on page 240)

2 tablespoons extra-virgin olive oil, divided

1 cup diced onions

2 cups Arborio rice (No substitutions!)

salt & freshly ground black pepper to taste

1 cup Chardonnay or other full-bodied, dry white wine

20 threads of saffron (approximately)

1 pound baby shrimp (60 to 70 count), peeled and deveined

2 shallots, minced

$1/2$ cup sherry

2 scallions, sliced $1/8$ inch on the bias

$1^3/4$ pounds ripe tomatoes, peeled, seeded, and diced, to make 2 cups

1 cup freshly grated Reggiano Parmesan cheese

Heat the stock in a saucepan.

In a heavy-bottom soup kettle (approximately 12 inches in diameter and 4 to 6 inches deep), heat 1 tablespoon of the olive oil and when hot, add the onions. When the onions become translucent and a light golden brown, add the rice, salt, and pepper. Toss the rice constantly until the grains turn light gold in color. Add the wine and the saffron. When all the wine has been absorbed by the rice, add enough stock to barely cover the rice. Simmer very slowly until all the stock has been absorbed. Continue adding the stock, 1 cup at a time, allowing the stock to be absorbed completely between each addition.

In the meantime, in a sauté pan, heat the remaining 1 tablespoon olive oil and add the shrimp and shallots. Cook for 2 minutes and add the sherry. Cook for 2 more minutes. Stir in the scallions and tomatoes.

After all the stock has been absorbed into the rice, stir in the shrimp mixture. When all remaining liquid has been absorbed, adjust the seasoning with salt and pepper, if needed. Stir in the Parmesan cheese. Serve immediately.

Wild Mushroom Risotto

OFTEN when I'm working in the office, I'll take a half hour and go over to the cooking school kitchen and make myself a risotto. There's really nothing like it! If you do it right, the risotto will be creamy, but not a paste. You'll still be able to taste every grain of the rice.

makes 4 servings

6 cups (approximately) Chicken Stock (recipe on page 240)

3 tablespoons extra-virgin olive oil, divided

1 cup finely diced onions

2 cups Arborio rice (No substitutions!)

salt & freshly ground black pepper to taste

1 cup Chardonnay or other full-bodied, dry white wine

2 shallots, freshly diced

1 1/2 pounds cremini (or mixed wild) mushrooms, sliced

1/2 cup port wine

1 cup freshly grated Reggiano Parmesan cheese

Heat the stock in a saucepan.

In a heavy-bottom soup kettle (approximately 12 inches in diameter and 4 to 6 inches deep), heat 2 tablespoons of olive oil and when hot, add the onions. When the onions become a light golden brown, add the rice, salt, and pepper. Toss the rice constantly until the grains turn light gold in color. Add the wine and when all the wine has been absorbed by the rice, add 1 cup stock. Simmer very slowly until all the stock has been absorbed. Continue adding the stock, 1 cup at a time, allowing the stock to be absorbed completely between each addition.

In the meantime, in a sauté pan, heat the remaining 1 tablespoon olive oil, add the shallots and sweat them for 2 minutes. Add the mushrooms and cook for 2 minutes. Add the port wine and 1/2 cup stock. Let simmer for 5 minutes.

Return to the rice and add more stock until all has been absorbed. Continue to stir slowly.

Add the mushroom mixture and continue to stir until almost all the liquid has been absorbed.

Adjust the seasoning with salt and pepper, if needed. Stir in the Parmesan cheese. Serve immediately.

poultry

E ven before I adopted a lower-fat, healthier style of cooking and eating, chicken was one of the foods I enjoyed most—and prepared most often. And why not? It's almost universally popular, inexpensive, and versatile.

But that's the problem with it, too! Perhaps like many of you, I have chicken at least once or twice each week, which means I am always looking for new ways to make it. In this chapter, I share with you over a dozen of my all-time favorite chicken recipes, but I must tell you: If you are going to try only one, make it the Coq au Vin (page 108). This is a low-fat version of that popular classic, and now it is without a doubt my number one poultry recipe. I am certain it will become one of your favorites, too.

I must add a word about the proper way to buy and store chicken. When you shop, buy your poultry last, and pack your frozen vegetables and other cold foods around it in the cart. Go right home after you finish at the market; don't leave the groceries thawing in the car while you do other errands. And once you get home, put them away immedi-

ately in the refrigerator or freezer. Also, thoroughly clean your cutting boards and utensils—and your hands. It is relatively easy for poultry to become contaminated with bacteria—but it is also relatively easy to avoid, if you're careful.

Coq au Vin (Chicken in Red Wine)

IF you try only one recipe in this entire book, it should be this one. It is so simple. I know that after you make it the first time, you'll cook it over and over again. Remember to leave the chicken on the bone!

makes 8 servings

$^1\!/_2$ cup all-purpose flour

$^1\!/_2$ teaspoon salt

$^1\!/_2$ teaspoon freshly ground black pepper

3 tablespoons extra-virgin olive oil, divided

4 chicken breasts, bone-in, skinless and cut in half

4 chicken legs, bone-in, skinless and cut in half

1 cup pearl onions, fresh or frozen

$^1\!/_4$ pound small fresh button mushrooms (quartered, if they are larger than $^1\!/_2$ inch in diameter)

1 slice 97% fat-free smoked ham, cut into $^1\!/_4$-inch cubes

1 tablespoon chopped fresh garlic

$^1\!/_2$ cup brandy

1 tablespoon chopped fresh thyme leaves

2 cups Cabernet Sauvignon or other full-bodied red wine

$^1\!/_2$ cup Chicken Stock (recipe on page 240)

2 tablespoons tomato paste

2 bay leaves

salt & freshly ground black pepper to taste

2 tablespoons chopped fresh parsley

Combine the flour, salt, and pepper on a large plate. Dredge the chicken pieces in the flour.

In a large Dutch oven (with a lid), heat 2 tablespoons of the olive oil. Brown the chicken pieces until golden brown on all sides. Remove the chicken pieces and set aside. Wipe the pan clean with a paper towel.

In the same pot, heat the remaining 1 tablespoon olive oil, add the pearl onions and sauté until golden brown. Add the mushrooms and ham and sauté for 2 minutes. Add the garlic and, when fragrant, add the brandy and thyme and reduce for 2 minutes. Add the red wine, stock, tomato paste, and bay leaves. Bring to a simmer and add the chicken pieces. Cover and cook slowly for about 35 minutes, or until chicken meat comes off the bone easily.

Remove the bay leaves. Adjust the seasoning with salt and pepper to taste. Sprinkle with chopped parsley. Serve with mashed potatoes or egg noodles.

Roasted Turkey with Cornbread & Sausage Stuffing

makes 12 servings

one 9-pound turkey

salt & freshly ground black pepper

2 tablespoons chopped fresh sage or 1 tablespoon dried rubbed sage

2 tablespoons chopped fresh thyme or 1 tablespoon dried thyme leaves

2 tablespoons chopped fresh rosemary or 1 tablespoon dried

2 Granny Smith apples, cut into chunks

2 large yellow onions, cut into chunks

2 large oranges, cut into chunks

1 celery stalk, cut into chunks

Giblet & Apple Brandy Gravy (recipe on page 252)

Preheat oven to 350°F.

Pat the turkey dry with paper towels. Season the inside with salt and pepper. Sprinkle the inside and the outside with the herbs. Stuff the inside of the bird with the apples, onions, oranges, and celery. Tie the legs together loosely to hold the shape of the turkey.

Place the turkey in a large roasting pan. Do not cover the turkey. Roast until a meat thermometer inserted into the thickest part registers 180°F. The juices should run clear. (For a 9-pound turkey, roast for approximately 3 hours.)

Remove turkey from the oven and tent with foil. Wait 30 minutes before carving. Serve with the Giblet & Apple Brandy Gravy.

cornbread & sausage stuffing

1 cup dark raisins

1/2 cup port wine

1/4 cup B&B liqueur (or brandy)

1 pound low-fat, sweet Italian sausage, casings removed

2 cups finely diced yellow onions

2 cups finely diced celery hearts

1 tablespoon chopped fresh sage

1 tablespoon chopped fresh rosemary

2 tablespoons chopped fresh thyme

6 cups low-fat cornbread or low-fat corn muffin crumbs

1 1/2 cups roasted and peeled (or canned) chestnuts

1 cup finely diced Granny Smith apples

1 cup fresh parsley, chopped

salt & freshly ground black pepper to taste

2 cups Chicken Stock (recipe on page 240)

Preheat oven to 350°F.

Soak the raisins in the port and B&B for at least 2 hours or, preferably, overnight.

In a large sauté pan over high heat, sauté the sausage. Drain excess fat. Add the onions and sweat them for 2 minutes. Add the celery and sauté for 2 to 3 minutes, then add all the fresh herbs. Transfer to a large bowl. Add all the remaining ingredients, including the soaked raisins.

Spray a baking pan or dish (approximately 15 inches x 10 inches x 2 inches) with a vegetable oil spray. Place the stuffing in the baking pan, cover with foil, and bake for 45 minutes. Uncover and bake for 15 more minutes, or until the top is golden brown.

Cilantro Chicken in a Pot

I could eat chicken and rice almost every day. This is a wonderful and VERY EASY recipe. Be sure to sauté the pieces until golden brown, and don't forget the olives; they are key! The cilantro may be substituted with Italian parsley (if you really must).

makes 6 servings

1 tablespoon extra-virgin olive oil

one 4-pound chicken, cut into 8 pieces, skin removed

1 cup minced white onions

1 red bell pepper, cut into brunoise (tiny dice)

¼ pound mushrooms, sliced

1 tablespoon minced fresh garlic

½ cup Chardonnay or other full-bodied, dry white wine

¼ cup brandy

1 cup short-grain rice

1½ cups Chicken Stock (recipe on page 240)

½ cup stuffed green olives, chopped

½ cup chopped fresh cilantro leaves

salt & freshly ground black pepper to taste

In a large soup kettle or Dutch oven, heat the olive oil. When hot, sauté the chicken pieces until golden brown on all sides. Remove from pot and set aside.

Add the onions to the kettle and when translucent, add the peppers, mushrooms, and garlic. When the garlic is fragrant, pour in the wine and brandy. Add the rice and mix well. Add the stock, the reserved chicken pieces, the olives, and cilantro. Season with salt and pepper to taste.

Cover and cook on low heat for 20 minutes. Uncover and cook for 5 to 10 more minutes, until liquid is completely absorbed.

Sesame Chicken Breasts with Ginger & Lime Sauce

IT is very important to pound the chicken to ¼ inch thick; otherwise, the sesame seeds will burn, while the inside of the chicken will still be rare.

makes 4 servings

four 6- to 8-ounce boneless, skinless chicken breasts

¼ cup white sesame seeds for dredging

salt & freshly ground black pepper to taste

1 tablespoon extra-virgin olive oil

1 cup bean sprouts

1 cup snow peas

¼ cup sugar

¼ cup freshly squeezed lime juice

1 teaspoon grated fresh ginger

¼ cup rice-wine vinegar

½ cup Chicken Stock (recipe on page 240)

½ cup sake (Japanese rice wine)

1 tablespoon low-sodium soy sauce

1 tablespoon cornstarch mixed with 2 tablespoons water (optional, for thickening)

Place the chicken breasts between two sheets of plastic wrap or wax paper and pound each one to ¼ inch thick scaloppine style. Dredge each scaloppine in the sesame seeds and season with salt and pepper.

Heat the olive oil in a large nonstick sauté pan. Sauté the sesame-coated chicken until golden brown on both sides. Remove the chicken and set aside. In the same pan, add the bean sprouts and the snow peas. Quickly sauté for 2 minutes.

In a saucepan, combine the sugar, lime juice, vinegar, and ginger and cook until the mixture is reduced by half. Add the stock, sake, and soy sauce. Season with salt and pepper. Reduce for 15 minutes and add to the vegetables. If you like, thicken the sauce with the cornstarch mixture and cook about 1 minute.

Combine the sauce with the chicken and toss well.

Chicken Breasts with Apricot, Grand Marnier & Basil

MARINATING the apricots in Grand Marnier makes them so succulent and tender! You could also use Curaçao, if you wish; it would be just as good. The marriage of basil and pine nuts also helps to create the outstanding flavor in this recipe, which tastes so elegant but is really very simple. As long as you leave enough time for the marinating, you can prepare the rest one, two, three!

makes 4 servings

6 ounces dried apricots, chopped

¼ cup Grand Marnier, Curaçao or other orange liqueur

1 tablespoon extra-virgin olive oil

four 6- to 8-ounce boneless, skinless chicken breasts

½ cup Chicken Stock (recipe on page 240)

2 tablespoons fresh basil sliced into chiffonade (thin ribbons)

2 tablespoons toasted pine nuts

1 tablespoon chopped shallots

1 cup snow peas

¼ cup rice-wine vinegar

1 tablespoon grated fresh ginger

salt & freshly ground black pepper to taste

Marinate the apricots in the liqueur for at least 2 hours.

Preheat oven to 425°F.

In an ovenproof sauté pan, heat 2 teaspoons of the olive oil, sear the chicken breasts until golden brown on all sides. Transfer the pan to the oven, cooking for 5 to 7 minutes.

In the meantime, in a saucepan, heat the remaining 1 teaspoon olive oil and sweat the shallots until light golden brown. Add the snow peas, quickly sauté for 2 minutes. Add the rice-wine vinegar and reduce by half. Add the stock, basil, pine nuts, ginger, and the marinated apricots.

Adjust the seasoning with salt and pepper.

Chicken Breasts in a Port & Raisin Sauce

I love this creamy sauce. Nutmeg is the signature ingredient, but the raisins bring a very important texture and sweetness. This sauce would also taste fantastic with veal chops, pork chops, or pork tenderloin. My Diced Potatoes & Onions (recipe on page 205) makes a nice accompaniment.

makes 4 servings

1/2 cup dark raisins

1 cup port wine

2 tablespoons extra-virgin olive oil, divided

four 6- to 8-ounce boneless, skinless chicken breasts

2 shallots, diced

1/4 pound fresh mushrooms, sliced

2 tablespoons balsamic vinegar

1 cup evaporated skim milk

1/4 teaspoon grated fresh nutmeg

1 tablespoon cornstarch mixed with 1 tablespoon water

salt & freshly ground black pepper to taste

fresh herbs for garnish

Soak the raisins in the port wine at least 1 hour or, preferably, overnight.

Preheat oven to 375°F.

In a sauté pan, heat 1 tablespoon of the olive oil. When hot, sauté the chicken breasts on one side until golden brown. Turn the chicken over and transfer to an ovenproof dish. Bake for 10 minutes.

In the meantime, in the sauté pan, heat the remaining 1 tablespoon olive oil. Add the shallots and sweat them for 2 minutes. Add the mushrooms and sauté them for 2 minutes. Add the vinegar and reduce until almost dry.

Stir in the raisins and their soaking liquid. Cook until the liquid is reduced by half. Add the evaporated milk, nutmeg, and cornstarch mixture. Cook for 2 more minutes, but do not bring to a boil.

Adjust the seasoning with salt and pepper. Spoon the sauce onto serving plates, set a chicken breast on top, and garnish with fresh herbs.

Chicken Tenderloins with Mushrooms, Artichoke Hearts & Cherry Tomatoes

THIS is a very clean and fresh dish—perfect for a summertime lunch.

makes 4 servings

1 tablespoon extra-virgin olive oil

24 ounces chicken tenderloins OR four 6-ounce boneless, skinless breasts, cut into $1/2$-inch-wide strips

$1/2$ red bell pepper, julienne

$1/2$ yellow bell pepper, julienne

2 scallions, cut on the diagonal into $3/4$-inch pieces

$1/4$ pound button mushrooms, sliced

1 tablespoon chopped fresh garlic

8 ounces artichoke hearts, quartered

1 cup Chicken Stock (recipe on page 240)

$1/2$ cup sherry

1 tablespoon cornstarch, mixed with 1 tablespoon water

salt & freshly ground black pepper to taste

1 dozen cherry tomatoes, cut into quarters

2 tablespoons chopped fresh parsley

In a deep sauté pan or a wok, heat the olive oil. When hot, add the chicken pieces. When golden brown on all sides, add the peppers and scallions. Cook for 2 minutes. Add the mushrooms and garlic. When the garlic becomes fragrant, add the artichokes, stock, sherry, and cornstarch mixture. Bring to a boil and adjust the seasoning with salt and pepper. Add the tomatoes and parsley.

Chicken with Coconut, Curry & Cinnamon Sauce

THIS excellent curry sauce is thickened with apples and bananas. The flavor is absolutely wonderful!

makes 6 servings

four 6-ounce boneless, skinless chicken breasts

2 tablespoons extra-virgin olive oil, divided

$1/4$ cup chopped yellow onions

$1/4$ cup chopped leeks

1 tablespoon medium hot curry powder

1 teaspoon finely chopped fresh ginger

$1/4$ cup rice-wine vinegar

$1/2$ cup Chardonnay or other full-bodied, dry white wine

1 cup Chicken Stock (recipe on page 240)

1 yellow apple, peeled, cored, and cut into $1/4$-inch cubes

1 medium banana, cut into 1-inch chunks

5 tablespoons coconut milk

1 stick cinnamon

1 pound tomatoes, peeled, seeded, and chopped, to make 1 cup

salt & ground white pepper to taste

Cut chicken breasts into $1^{1}/2$- to 2-inch chunks. Heat 1 tablespoon of the olive oil in a sauté pan. Brown chicken pieces on all sides, then cook on very low heat until done, about 5 to 7 minutes.

In a saucepan, heat the remaining 1 tablespoon olive oil and add the onions and leeks. When they become translucent, add the curry and ginger. Add the rice-wine vinegar and let reduce until almost dry. Pour in the wine and let reduce by half. Add the stock, the apples, bananas, coconut milk, and cinnamon and cook for 15 minutes. Remove the cinnamon stick.

With an immersion blender, or in a regular blender, purée the sauce to a very smooth consistency. Add the tomatoes and the chicken pieces and adjust the seasonings.

Serve with freshly wilted spinach and basmati rice.

Chicken Breasts Stuffed with Herb Cream Cheese & Smoked Ham on a Bed of Arugula

ORIGINALLY this recipe called for Boursin cheese, so to reduce the fat, I made a mixture of cream cheese, garlic, and fresh herbs. It tastes even better than the Boursin, and it's lower in fat! You must secure the stuffed chicken with toothpicks to ensure a tight roll.

makes 6 servings

four 6-ounce boneless, skinless chicken breasts

¼ teaspoon salt

¼ teaspoon freshly ground black pepper

4 thin slices 97% fat-free smoked ham

8 ounces Herb Cream Cheese (recipe on page 247)

1 tablespoon extra-virgin olive oil

Mustard & Balsamic Vinaigrette (recipe on page 248)

2 bunches arugula, washed and dried

Preheat oven to 375°F.

Place the chicken breasts between two pieces of clear plastic wrap or wax paper. Pound each to ¼ inch thick. Discard the wrap and season each breast with salt and pepper on both sides.

Lay a slice of ham on each breast. Spoon a 2-inch strip of the Herb Cream Cheese along the bottom edge of each chicken breast. Fold in and roll the chicken firmly, until you have a tight roll. Secure with toothpicks to hold a tight roll.

In an ovenproof sauté pan, heat the olive oil and sear each chicken roll until golden brown on all sides. Transfer the pan to the oven and bake the rolls for 10 minutes.

In the meantime, make the Mustard & Balsamic Vinaigrette. Toss the arugula with the vinaigrette until all leaves glisten.

Cover the bottom of a plate with the tossed arugula. Place a chicken roll in the middle and serve immediately. You may slice the roll into 4 or 5 slices for a more decorative presentation.

Stir-Fried Chicken with Wild Mushrooms & Asparagus

WHEN you come home from work and want something quick and delicious, this is the recipe to use. The meat and vegetable combination is wonderful, and nothing could be faster than stir-frying in a wok. The hoisin sauce, widely used in Chinese cooking, can be found in Asian markets and most large supermarkets.

makes 6 servings

1 tablespoon extra-virgin olive oil

four 6- to 8-ounce boneless, skinless chicken breasts, cut into $1/2$- x $1^1/2$-inch strips

1 pound pencil-thin asparagus spears, cut on the diagonal into 1-inch pieces

$1/2$ pound mixed wild mushrooms (cremini, shiitake, etc.), sliced

$3/4$ cup Chicken Stock (recipe on page 240)

$1/4$ cup rice-wine vinegar

2 tablespoons ketchup

1 tablespoon soy sauce

1 teaspoon chili sauce

1 tablespoon hoisin sauce

In a deep sauté pan or a wok, heat the olive oil. Add the chicken and sauté until golden brown on all sides. Add the asparagus and sauté for 2 minutes. Add the mushrooms and sauté 2 more minutes. Add the stock, vinegar, ketchup, soy sauce, chili sauce, and hoisin sauce. Mix well and serve immediately with wild rice or brown rice.

incredible cuisine

Chicken & Apples in a Pot

As the apple cooks inside the chicken, it develops a wonderful sweetness that complements the fresh rosemary and thyme beautifully!

makes 8 servings

- one 4- to 5-pound roasting chicken, skin and excess fat removed
- salt & freshly ground black pepper to taste
- 2 green apples, cut into 4 pieces
- 6 sprigs fresh thyme
- 6 sprigs fresh rosemary
- 1 whole garlic head, cut in half crosswise
- 1 tablespoon extra-virgin olive oil
- 1 cup fresh pearl onions, peeled
- 1/2 cup diced Canadian bacon
- 2 cups small nouvelle potatoes, cut into 1-inch cubes
- 1 cup baby carrots
- 1 cup small button mushrooms
- 1 tablespoon chopped fresh garlic
- 3 cups Chicken Stock (recipe on page 240)
- 1 cup Chardonnay or other full-bodied, dry white wine

Preheat oven to 400°F.

Season the chicken inside and out with salt and pepper. Tuck the cut apples, 2 sprigs of rosemary, 2 sprigs of thyme, and garlic head inside the cavity.

Heat the olive oil in a large ovenproof casserole with a lid (large enough to hold the chicken) on the stovetop. Add the pearl onions and sauté until golden brown. Add the Canadian bacon and cook 2 more minutes. Add the potatoes, carrots, mushrooms, and chopped garlic. Place the chicken in the casserole, breast side up, on top of the vegetables. Pour in the stock and wine. Add the remaining sprigs of thyme and rosemary. Bring the liquid to a boil.

Cover the casserole and transfer it to the bottom rack of the oven. Make sure the liquid bubbles very softly and does not boil. Cook for 1 1/4 hours, or until the juice runs transparent (without a trace of pink) when the meat is pierced with a fork.

Roast Duck with Chile Pepper Glaze

EVERYONE is always afraid of cooking duck, but there's nothing to it! And if you do it properly, you can get rid of a lot of the fat.

makes 2 servings

one 4½- to 5-pound Long Island duckling, fresh or frozen

salt & freshly ground black pepper to taste

1 green apple, cut into cubes

1 orange, quartered

1 large onion, peeled and chopped into 8 pieces

1 sprig fresh rosemary

1 sprig fresh thyme

Chile Pepper Glaze (recipe on page 260)

Note: If the duckling is frozen, thaw it slowly in the refrigerator, allowing at least 24 hours. Forty-eight hours is even better! Don't use the running water method as the meat becomes tough and dry if you rush the defrosting. Fresh is great, if you can get it.

Preheat oven to 400°F.

Remove the neck, heart, and liver from inside the duckling and rinse the bird well under cold running water. Drain and turn upside down for a few minutes so all excess water runs out. Cut off the wing tips and reserve with the neck and giblets. Trim off excess skin and visible fat from the neck and body cavities. Season the duck inside and out with salt and pepper. Tuck the liver, the apples, oranges, onions, and herbs inside the body cavity.

Place a wire rack in the bottom of the roasting pan. If you do not have a rack, cover the bottom of the pan with apples cut in half (cut side down) and place the duck on top, with breast side up. Roast for 45 minutes.

Reverse the position of the roasting pan (that is, turn it back to front) and cook for 45 more minutes. For a nice medium to medium-rare duck, the juice runs slightly pink when the thigh meat is pierced. Even if you like your duck well done, you should take it from the oven medium, as it will cook more when you reheat it after you have made the sauce. The juice will be clear when the duck is well done. Remove from the oven and let cool.

Using a sharp, boning knife and starting at the neck, remove each half from the bone in one piece by scraping carefully back, making sure the knife's edge is held against the bone while you pull away the meat gently with your other hand. Repeat with the other half.

After you have made the sauce and you are ready to serve, preheat the broiler to 500°F. Place the carved-up duck halves on a baking pan and place under the broiler to reheat for 3 to 4 minutes to crisp the skin.

Baked Chicken Pinot Noir

THIS also makes a fantastic chicken and pasta dish. Just cut the chicken in strips instead of leaving the breasts whole.

makes 4 servings

2 tablespoons extra-virgin olive oil, divided

1 cup sliced onions

1 medium red bell pepper, sliced into 8 pieces

1 medium green bell pepper, sliced into 8 pieces

2 cups Pinot Noir or other fruity, dry, red wine

1/4 cup apple-cider vinegar

1 cup Chicken Stock (recipe on page 240)

1 tablespoon cornstarch mixed with 1 tablespoon water

4 bone-in, skinless chicken breasts

flour seasoned with salt & pepper, for dredging

2 tomatoes, each cut into 8 slices

8 garlic cloves

4 sprigs fresh rosemary

4 sprigs fresh thyme

Preheat oven to 375°F.

In a saucepan, heat 1 tablespoon of the olive oil and add the onions. Sweat them for 2 minutes then add the peppers. Cook for 2 minutes. Add the wine and vinegar and let reduce for 5 minutes on medium-high heat. Add the stock and cornstarch mixture. Cook for an additional 2 minutes.

In the meantime, dredge the chicken breasts in the seasoned flour. In a sauté pan, heat the remaining 1 tablespoon olive oil and sear the chicken breasts until golden brown.

Transfer the chicken to an ovenproof dish. Place the tomato slices between the chicken breasts. Add the garlic cloves and fresh herbs. Pour the sauce over the chicken, cover, and bake for 35 minutes.

Chicken Tenderloins with Pear & Ginger Sauce

THIS is a quick and very interesting recipe using two unique ingredients—pears and cabbage. What a wonderful combination! Not to worry if the pears are not quite ripe. As a matter of fact, it is better if they're underripe, as they will retain a certain texture that complements the cabbage perfectly.

makes 6 servings

1 tablespoon extra-virgin olive oil

1 1/2 pounds chicken tenderloins, or boneless, skinless breasts, cut into 1/2-inch-wide strips

1 pear, peeled, cored, and cut into 1/8-inch julienne

1 cup red cabbage sliced 1/4 inch into chiffonade (1/4-inch-wide ribbons)

1 scallion cut on the diagonal into pieces 3/4 inch long

2 tablespoons sugar dissolved in 2 tablespoons red wine vinegar

1/2 cup Chicken Stock (recipe on page 240)

1/4 cup Chardonnay or other full-bodied, dry white wine

2 tablespoons chopped walnuts (optional)

1 tablespoon grated fresh ginger

1 tablespoon cornstarch, mixed with 2 tablespoons water

salt & freshly ground black pepper to taste

In a deep sauté pan or a wok, heat the olive oil. When hot, add the chicken strips and the julienne pears. When the chicken is golden brown on all sides, add the cabbage and scallions. Cook for 2 minutes, then add the vinegar with sugar and reduce for 2 minutes. Add the stock, wine, walnuts, and ginger and reduce for 2 additional minutes. Add the cornstarch mixture to thicken the sauce, if necessary.

Season with salt and pepper.

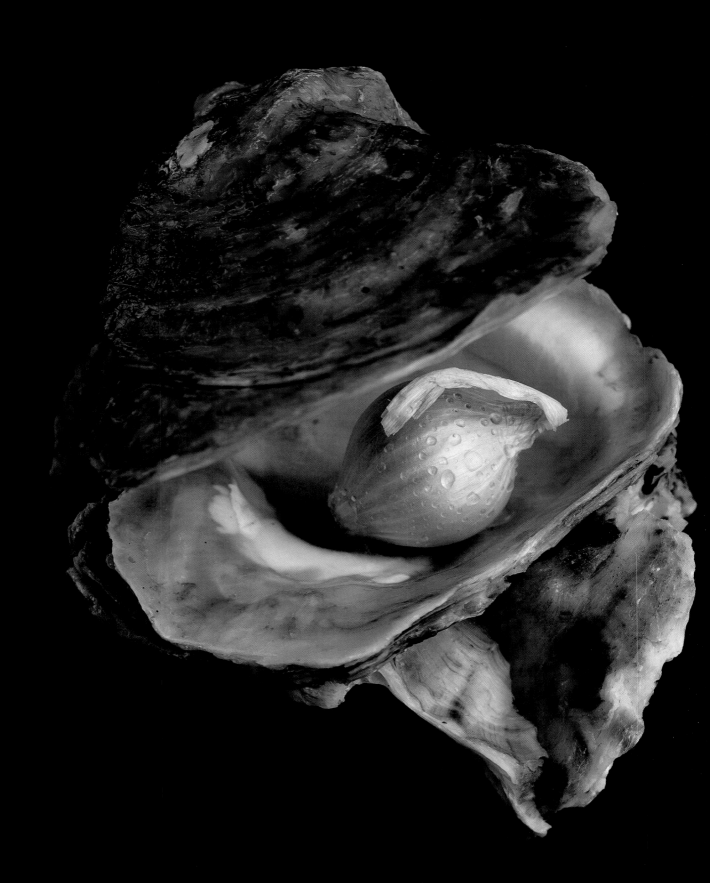

fish & shellfish

One of the great joys of living where I do, in South Florida, is the variety of fish and shellfish available every day in our markets, all year round. We are spoiled, I know! This is why so many seafood dishes appear on the menu at my restaurant, and why I often prepare fish at home, too. When it's this fresh, it's hard to resist.

But many people tell me they do not like to cook fish at home, and they say it's because they're not sure how to do it properly. What's the single biggest mistake most people make with fish? They overcook it. They cook it until it becomes dry and rubbery, when it should be moist and flaky. Follow my cooking instructions carefully, and you will get much better results—I promise!

You'll notice that many of my recipes are for coatings with surprising ingredients—couscous, cornmeal and pecan, potatoes. That's because I love to create a crunchy texture on fish. It makes for a little excitement in the presentation. But any one of these recipes would be fine without a crust, too. There's absolutely nothing like a piece of just-caught fish, whisked under the broiler, and drizzled with lemon juice. Delicious!

Cajun-Spiced Mahi-Mahi

SERVE this with the Goat Cheese Polenta (recipe on page 201) and the Kalamata Olive Sauce (recipe on page 244), and you'll agree that the different textures and flavors in this dish are absolutely incredible. Grouper, sea bass, or swordfish could replace the mahi-mahi.

makes 4 servings

four 6- to 8-ounce mahi-mahi (dolphin) fillets

2 tablespoons extra-virgin olive oil

Kalamata Olive Sauce (recipe on page 244)

Prepare the Blackening Seasoning per the recipe below.

To cook the fish fillets, preheat oven to 375°F. Pat dry each fish fillet. Dredge each fillet in the Blackening Seasoning on the top side only (the opposite of the skin side). Tap each fillet to remove any excess seasoning. In a nonstick, ovenproof frying pan, heat the olive oil. When hot, carefully place the fillets into the pan, seasoned side down. Cook for 3 to 4 minutes, shaking pan to make sure the seasoning does not stick.

Using a large spatula, flip each fillet over. Transfer the pan to the oven, and bake for 4 to 5 minutes (slightly longer if fillets are over 1 inch thick), or until cooked to your liking.

blackening seasoning

1 tablespoon cayenne pepper

1 tablespoon dried thyme leaves

1 tablespoon red pepper flakes

$1/2$ tablespoon paprika

$1/4$ teaspoon ground sage

$1/4$ teaspoon ground coriander

$1/4$ teaspoon salt

$1/4$ teaspoon freshly ground black pepper

Blend all the seasonings, using a small food processor or coffee grinder.

Yellowtail Snapper with Mango-Tequila Sauce

HOLY macaroli—this fish is so, so easy! And don't worry if you can't get the snapper or the mangoes. Catfish, orange roughy, or sole would also work, and you can substitute papaya, peaches, or even apricots for the mangoes. If tarragon wine vinegar is hard to find, use a good white wine vinegar.

makes 4 servings

four 6-ounce snapper fillets, skinned

1 cup cornmeal

2 tablespoons extra-virgin olive oil, divided

2 shallots, chopped fine

3 tablespoons tarragon wine vinegar

$^1/_4$ cup tequila

1 cup Chicken Stock (recipe on page 240)

$^1/_4$ cup orange juice concentrate

1$^1/_2$ cups diced mangoes

2 tablespoons snipped fresh chives

salt & freshly ground black pepper to taste

Preheat oven to 375°F.

Dip each fish fillet in the cornmeal and dust off excess.

In an ovenproof sauté pan large enough to hold the fillets without crowding, heat 1 tablespoon of the olive oil. Add the snapper and sauté for 1 minute. Turn fillets over, then transfer the pan to the oven, and bake the fish for 4 to 5 minutes. The fish should then be opaque, not translucent.

While the fish is baking, in a medium saucepan, heat 1 tablespoon olive oil. Sweat the shallots and when translucent, add the vinegar. Let reduce until almost dry. Add the tequila and let reduce by half. Stir in the stock, orange juice concentrate, and mangoes. Let simmer for 5 minutes.

Pour into blender and process until very smooth. Add the chives and adjust the seasoning.

For a beautiful presentation, spoon about 2 tablespoons sauce onto a dinner plate and set the cooked fish in the center. Cut a mango into small cubes, or decorate with purple basil and chives. Arrange diced mango in the sauce.

Couscous-Crusted Mahi-Mahi with Mixed Vegetable Casserole

THIS interesting couscous crust will become one of your favorites! It is virtually foolproof to prepare. Be sure to pack it onto the fish at least $1/4$ inch thick.

makes 4 servings

2 cups cooked couscous (recipe below)

four 6- to 8-ounce mahi-mahi (dolphin) fillets

$1/2$ cup all-purpose flour for dredging

salt & ground white pepper to taste

2 egg substitutes

1 tablespoon extra-virgin olive oil

3 cups Mixed Vegetable Casserole (recipe on page 194)

Cook the couscous. Preheat oven to 350°F.

Pat dry the snapper fillets. Dredge each fillet in seasoned flour. Pat each fillet to remove any excess flour.

Using a paintbrush, generously paint the egg onto the top side (the opposite of the skin side) of each fillet. Firmly press the couscous onto each fillet in an even layer approximately $1/4$ inch thick.

In a nonstick, ovenproof frying pan, heat the olive oil. When hot, carefully place the fillets into the pan, crust side down. Cook for 3 to 4 minutes, shaking pan to make sure the couscous does not stick.

Using a large spatula, flip each fillet over to the other side and bake in the oven, couscous side up, for 3 to 4 minutes (a little longer if fillets are over 1 inch thick), or until the fish is cooked to your liking.

Couscous

makes 2 cups cooked

$1 1/4$ cups water

2 tablespoons extra-virgin olive oil

$1/2$ teaspoon salt

1 garlic clove, chopped fine

1 cup couscous

In a saucepan, bring the water, olive oil, salt, and garlic to a rolling boil. Add the couscous and immediately remove from the heat. Stir and let it stand for 5 minutes. Fluff with a fork.

Cornmeal & Pecan-Crusted Red Snapper

THE pecan and cornmeal give the fish a rich, nutty flavor and texture.

makes 4 servings

- $1/2$ cup cornmeal
- $1/4$ cup all-purpose flour
- 2 tablespoons pecans
- 3 tablespoons extra-virgin olive oil, divided
- four 6-ounce red snapper fillets, skinned and boned
- 2 shallots, minced
- $1/2$ red bell pepper, cut into brunoise (diced very small)
- $1/2$ green bell pepper, cut into brunoise
- $1/2$ yellow bell pepper, cut into brunoise
- $1/4$ Scotch bonnet chile pepper, seeded and cut into brunoise
- $1/2$ fennel bulb, trimmed and cut into brunoise
- $1/4$ cup rice-wine vinegar
- $1/2$ cup Chicken Stock (recipe on page 240)
- 2 tablespoons Pernod liqueur
- $1/4$ cup evaporated milk
- 1 tablespoon cornstarch mixed with 2 tablespoons water
- salt & ground white pepper to taste
- 2 cups spinach leaves, washed and dried

Preheat oven to 375°F.

In a food processor, mix the cornmeal, flour, and pecans for 45 seconds (no longer, or it will get oily). Dredge each fish fillet in this mixture.

In a large ovenproof sauté pan (large enough to hold the fillets without crowding), heat 1 tablespoon of the olive oil. Add the snapper fillets, skin side down, and sauté for 1 minute, or until golden brown. Turn the fillets over, then transfer the pan to the oven to bake for 4 to 5 minutes.

While the fish is baking, prepare the sauce. In a medium saucepan, heat 1 tablespoon of the olive oil. Add the shallots and let them sweat until translucent. Add the bell peppers and Scotch bonnet chile. Allow them to sweat for 2 more minutes. Add the fennel and rice-wine vinegar. Let reduce until almost dry. Pour in the stock and Pernod. Bring to a boil, reduce heat, and stir in the milk. Add the cornstarch mixture, as necessary, to thicken. Season with salt and white pepper to taste. Turn the heat off and set the sauce aside.

In a sauté pan, heat the remaining 1 tablespoon olive oil. When hot, add the spinach, salt, and white pepper. Cook just long enough to wilt the spinach (no more than 2 minutes). Carefully cover the bottom of each plate with approximately $1/4$ cup of the sauce. Divide the spinach equally and place in the center of each serving plate. Then place a fish fillet on top of the spinach.

Black-Peppered Salmon
with Dill Mustard Sauce

THE freshly cracked black pepper creates a crunchy, beautiful crust on this salmon that not only looks impressive but also tastes outstanding. For a nice, coarse pepper, I wrap some peppercorns in a towel and smack them with a rolling pin or the flat side of a cleaver. You could also use an old coffee grinder—but not a peppermill: The pepper gets too finely ground.

makes 4 servings

four 5-ounce salmon fillets

3 tablespoons coarsely ground black pepper

2 tablespoons extra-virgin olive oil, divided

2 shallots, minced

$1/4$ cup rice-wine vinegar

$1/2$ cup Chardonnay or other full-bodied, dry white wine

$1/2$ cup bottled clam juice

$1/4$ cup evaporated milk

1 tablespoon cornstarch mixed with 1 tablespoon water

1 tablespoon Dijon mustard

1 tablespoon chopped fresh dill

salt & ground white pepper to taste

Preheat oven to 450°F.

Coat the top side of each salmon fillet with black pepper. In a nonstick sauté pan, heat 1 tablespoon of the olive oil. Sear one side of each fillet until golden brown, turn on the other side, and finish cooking in the oven for 4 to 5 more minutes.

In the meantime, in a saucepan, heat the remaining 1 tablespoon olive oil and when hot, sweat the shallots until light golden brown. Add the vinegar and reduce until almost dry. Pour in the wine and let reduce for 2 minutes. Add the clam juice and evaporated milk and cook for 2 minutes more. Stir in the cornstarch mixture to thicken, as desired. Strain through a fine sieve. Finally, add the mustard and dill. Season with salt and white pepper to taste.

Pour the sauce on the bottom of each plate and place a salmon fillet on top of the sauce.

Serve with Couscous (recipe on page 136) and snow peas.

Stir-Fried Shrimp with Snow Peas

THIS is a gorgeous-looking recipe, and so very simple to do. But it's the kind of dish that does not wait for you; plan on eating just as soon as it is completed. Mirin, or sweet rice wine, can be found in Japanese markets or the gourmet section of some supermarkets. Also, be sure to buy a high-quality sesame oil, one that actually smells like sesame seeds and has a slightly nutty flavor.

makes 4 servings

1 teaspoon sesame oil

1 pound medium shrimp (26 to 30 count), peeled and deveined

1 cup thinly sliced (chiffonade style) red cabbage

1 cup snow peas

1 teaspoon grated fresh ginger

1 teaspoon minced fresh garlic

$1/4$ cup dry sherry

$1/4$ cup bottled clam juice

2 tablespoons mirin (sweet Japanese cooking wine)

1 tablespoon oyster sauce

1 tablespoon low-sodium soy sauce

1 teaspoon cornstarch mixed with 1 teaspoon water

salt & freshly ground black pepper to taste

Heat the sesame oil in a nonstick frying pan. Add the shrimp and the red cabbage and sauté for 2 minutes. Add the snow peas, ginger, and garlic. When the garlic becomes fragrant, pour in the sherry and let reduce for 2 additional minutes. Add the clam juice, mirin, oyster sauce, soy sauce, and cornstarch mixture. Adjust the seasoning with salt and pepper.

Serve with rice pilaf.

Florida Bouillabaisse

THIS has become, by far, my favorite seafood dish. It does take some time to prepare, but it is the perfect thing for a big party. You can prepare the Bouillabaisse Stock the day before (or the week before and freeze it). Then, when your guests arrive, you just have to cook the seafood and prepare the garlic croutons. Make plenty, as everyone will go for seconds!

makes 8 servings

2 tablespoons extra-virgin olive oil

8 jumbo shrimp (15 count), peeled and deveined

6 small lobster tails, approximately 3 ounces each

24 clams, scrubbed

3 cups Bouillabaisse Stock (recipe on page 242)

8 ounces salmon, cut into large cubes

8 ounces snapper, cut into large cubes

8 ounces mahi-mahi (dolphin), cut into large cubes

$1/2$ pound baby shrimp

24 mussels, scrubbed

1 pound sea scallops (30 to 40 count)

garlic croutons for garnish

sliced star fruit (carambola) for garnish

In a stockpot, heat the olive oil and add the shrimp, lobster, and clams. Sauté for 3 to 4 minutes then add the Bouillabaisse Stock. Bring to a boil. Add the remaining seafood and cook for 5 minutes, or until all the seafood is cooked to your liking.

Divide the seafood equally among 4 large soup plates. Pour the stock over the seafood. Decorate the plate with garlic croutons and star fruit, if available.

Grilled Salmon with Green Peppercorn, Rum & Vanilla Sauce

WHEN I first came to Florida, I had used rum only in desserts. But over the years, as I've been developing recipes, I've discovered that rum is a wonderful liquor to use with fish. And I love the flavor combination of rum and vanilla—they were really meant to be together! The green peppercorns add a nice little kick. Served with grilled salmon, it couldn't get any better.

makes 4 servings

four 5-ounce salmon fillets

1 tablespoon extra-virgin olive oil

2 tablespoons minced shallots

1/2 cup Chardonnay or other full-bodied, dry white wine

2 tablespoons dark rum

1 cup evaporated skim milk

2 teaspoons green peppercorns

1 tablespoon pure vanilla extract

1 tablespoon tomato paste

1 tablespoon cornstarch mixed with 1 tablespoon water

salt & freshly ground black pepper to taste

Preheat grill to high heat or build a hot charcoal fire. Meanwhile, make the sauce.

In a saucepan, heat the olive oil and add the shallots. Cook until they are translucent. Then add the wine and let reduce by half. Add the rum and ignite with a match. When the flames subside, add the evaporated milk, peppercorns, vanilla, tomato paste, and the cornstarch mixture. Cook for 2 additional minutes, but do not bring to a boil. Adjust the seasoning with salt and pepper to taste.

Brush the grill with oil. Grill the salmon for 3 minutes, then turn over and cook another 3 minutes.

To serve, pour 2 tablespoons sauce on the bottom of each plate, arrange the grilled salmon on top.

Parmesan & Baby Shrimp-Crusted Yellowtail Snapper with Mango & Lime Sauce

MY friend, Chef Udo Mueller, invented this recipe when he was the chef at The Left Bank, and our guests fell in love with it. It is packed with flavor and texture.

makes 4 servings

2 tablespoons extra-virgin olive oil, divided

four 6- to 8-ounce yellowtail snapper fillets, skinned

2 tablespoons chopped shallots

1 teaspoon chopped fresh garlic

1/2 cup Chardonnay or other full-bodied, dry white wine

8 ounces tiny shrimp (90 to 110 count)

1/2 cup fresh bread crumbs made from white bread, crust removed

1/2 cup peeled, seeded and diced, tomatoes

1/2 cup freshly grated Reggiano Parmesan cheese

3 tablespoons low-fat sour cream

1 tablespoon chopped fresh dill

salt & freshly ground black pepper to taste

salt, pepper and flour for dusting

mango & lime sauce

2 overripe mangoes, peeled, seeded, and chopped

2 ounces dry vermouth

1/4 cup Chicken Stock (recipe on page 240)

1 teaspoon lime juice

Preheat oven to 425°F.

For the shrimp mixture, heat 1 tablespoon of the olive oil in a sauté pan and sauté the shallots until translucent. Add the garlic and when fragrant, pour in the wine. Add the shrimp and cook them until half done, approximately 2 minutes. Add the bread crumbs, half of the Parmesan cheese, the sour cream, and dill. Add the tomatoes and salt and pepper to taste. Set aside.

Dust the fillets with flour and pan sear in the remaining 1 tablespoon olive oil. Place the snapper on a nonstick baking sheet and top with the shrimp mixture. Sprinkle with the remaining Parmesan cheese. Bake in the preheated oven for 5 minutes. Switch oven to broil and finish until browned, approximately 2 minutes.

Make the Mango & Lime Sauce while the fish is cooking.

Spoon the sauce onto plates. Set the fish on top. Serve with couscous or rice pilaf and garnish with snow peas.

Place the mangoes, vermouth, stock, and lime juice in a blender and blend until smooth. Transfer to a saucepan and bring to a simmer. The sauce should not need any seasoning because of the sweetness from the mangoes, and the lime juice gives it the finishing touch.

incredible cuisine

Potato-Crusted Salmon with Chives & Scallion Sauce

T HIS presentation is absolutely stunning and so easy to achieve. Make sure the potatoes are pressed down firmly onto the fish, and use a nonstick frying pan.

makes 4 servings

2 large potatoes, peeled
four 4-ounce salmon fillets or steaks
salt & ground white pepper to taste
4 teaspoons Dijon mustard
1 tablespoon extra-virgin olive oil

Grate the potatoes using the large holes of the grater.

Pat the fish dry with paper towels. Season the fish lightly with salt and white pepper. Generously spread one side of each fillet or steak with the mustard (for fillets, spread mustard on the rounded side, not the skin side). Cover the mustard with enough grated potatoes to coat entirely. Cover the fish with plastic wrap and press the grated potatoes down onto the fish very firmly and tightly. Remove the wrap and season the potatoes with salt and white pepper.

Preheat oven to 425°F.

In an ovenproof, nonstick frying pan, heat the olive oil. When hot, place the fish very gently in the pan, with crust side down, using a large spatula to avoid breaking the crust. Sauté for 2 to 3 minutes until the potatoes are golden brown. Flip the fish carefully to the other side and finish cooking in the oven for about 5 minutes, or until the center of fillet is opaque in color.

Serve with the Chive & Scallion Sauce.

chive & scallion sauce

1 tablespoon extra-virgin olive oil
5 scallions, thinly sliced, white part only
1 tablespoon chopped fresh garlic
$1/4$ cup champagne vinegar
$1/2$ cup Chardonnay or other full-bodied, dry white wine
$1/2$ cup evaporated skim milk
1 teaspoon cornstarch mixed with 1 tablespoon water
6 chives, snipped
salt & ground white pepper to taste

In a saucepan, heat the olive oil then add the scallions and sauté for 2 minutes. Add the garlic and when fragrant, add the vinegar. Let reduce until almost dry. Pour in the wine and let reduce until half remains. Add the evaporated milk and the cornstarch mixture.

Remove from the heat as soon as it boils. Add the chives and adjust the seasoning with salt and white pepper.

Provençale Herb-Crusted Swordfish with Lemon-Caper Sauce

HERE classic Provençale flavors—herbs, lemon, and capers—are presented with a new twist: a delicious, fresh salad served underneath the fish. The contrast in texture and temperature is outstanding!

makes 4 servings

four 6-ounce swordfish fillets

2 egg whites, lightly beaten

2 cups bread crumbs, seasoned with *herbes de Provence* (thyme, oregano, rosemary and basil)

1 tablespoon extra-virgin olive oil

Place the fish fillets between 2 sheets of plastic wrap. Flatten to $^1/_2$ inch thick. Dip them in the beaten eggs whites, then in the seasoned bread crumbs. Heat the oil in a non-stick skillet. Cook the fish for 2 to 3 minutes on each side until golden brown.

Place romaine leaves, tossed with the Smoked Ham Relish, in the center of each serving plate. Then arrange the cooked swordfish on top of the greens. Pour some of the Lemon-Caper Sauce on top of the fish.

lemon-caper sauce

1 tablespoon extra-virgin olive oil

1 tablespoon finely chopped shallots

$^1/_2$ cup Chardonnay or other full-bodied, dry white wine

$^1/_4$ cup freshly squeezed lemon juice

1 cup Chicken Stock (recipe on page 240)

$^1/_4$ cup nonpareil (small) capers

$^1/_4$ cup chopped fresh parsley

$1^1/_2$ tablespoons cornstarch mixed with 1 tablespoon water

In a saucepan, heat the olive oil. Sweat the shallots, then add the wine and lemon juice and let reduce by half. Add the stock, capers, parsley, and cornstarch mixture. Bring to a boil and set aside.

chiffonade of romaine & radicchio with smoked ham relish

1 head romaine lettuce, sliced into chiffonade (thin ribbons, about $^1/_4$ inch)

1 head radicchio, sliced into chiffonade

$^1/_4$ cup Smoked Ham Relish (recipe on page 251)

Toss the romaine and radicchio with the Smoked Ham Relish.

Paella

I will not lie to you: There is no quick way to make a good paella. You will need to spend 2 or 3 hours in your kitchen. But I'll tell you, it is definitely worth every minute.

makes 8 servings

1 large red bell pepper for roasting

3 tablespoons extra-virgin olive oil, divided

¹/₂ pound veal tenderloin, cubed

¹/₂ pound pork tenderloin, cubed

¹/₂ pound 97% fat-free smoked ham, cubed ¹/₄ inch

8 to 10 pieces of skinless chicken (drumstick or breast), all fat removed

5 cups Chicken Stock (recipe on page 240)

1 generous tablespoon saffron threads

1 bay leaf

12 black peppercorns

8 jumbo shrimp (15 count), peeled and deveined

¹/₄ pound sea scallops

¹/₂ onion, chopped fine

1 tablespoon minced fresh garlic

1 red bell pepper, finely diced

1 green bell pepper, finely diced

1³/₄ pounds ripe tomatoes, peeled, seeded, and chopped, to make 2 cups OR one 28-ounce can recipe-ready tomatoes, drained

salt & freshly ground black pepper to taste

1¹/₂ cups Arborio rice

¹/₂ cup fresh or frozen peas

Preheat oven to 375°F.

Roast the bell pepper and cut into strips.

In a sauté pan, heat 1 tablespoon of the olive oil. When hot, sear the veal and pork until golden brown. Remove from pan. In the same pan, sauté the ham for 2 minutes and set aside. To the same pan, add the chicken and sauté until golden brown on all sides.

Pour the stock into a saucepan, add the saffron and reduce over medium-high heat for 10 minutes. Set aside. In another saucepan, heat 1 quart water with the bay leaf and peppercorns. When water comes to a boil, add the shrimp and let simmer for 4 minutes. Add the scallops and let simmer 2 more minutes. Remove the seafood.

In a saucepan, heat 1 tablespoon of the olive oil and add the onions. When translucent, add the garlic. When the garlic becomes fragrant, add the diced peppers and cook for 2 minutes. Add the tomatoes and the saffron-infused the stock and cook for 5 minutes. Add salt and pepper to taste.

In a large paella pan or sauté pan on top of the stove, heat the remaining 1 tablespoon olive oil. Sprinkle the uncooked rice and peas evenly in the pan. Place the cooked shrimp, pork, veal, ham, and chicken on top of the rice. Pour the tomato sauce mixture on top. Bring the paella to a boil, reduce the heat and let simmer on top of the stove for 5 minutes. Arrange the roasted bell pepper strips on top and bake for 15 to 20 minutes.

Serve immediately.

Key Lime Shrimp Brochette with Mango & Rum Salsa

THIS is perfect for a Sunday afternoon barbecue.

makes 4 servings

12 bamboo or wooden skewers

24 shrimp (20 to 25 count), peeled and deveined

$^1/_2$ cup fresh key lime or lemon juice

2 cups pineapple juice

$^1/_2$ cup dark rum

$^1/_4$ cup fresh cilantro, chopped

$^1/_2$ cup fresh green onions, chopped

2 tablespoons garlic, chopped

2 tablespoons apple cider vinegar

salt & freshly ground black pepper to taste

non-stick spray for grill

Soak 8 wooden or bamboo skewers for a minimum of 2 hours or preferably overnight. In a large glass bowl, stir together all the ingredients. Cover and refrigerate for at least 2 hours.

Preheat the grill, spray the grill with a non-stick spray. Place about 5 shrimp on each skewer and grill for 2 to 3 minutes on each side. You can also use 2 skewers, and it will be easier to manipulate on the grill.

To assemble, pour a quarter of the salsa on the bottom of each plate and place a shrimp brochette on top.

mango & rum salsa

2 ripe mangoes, cut into small cubes

2 scallions, chopped very fine

2 tablespoons fresh cilantro, chopped

1 tablespoon apple cider vinegar

1/2 cup fresh orange juice

1 dash Tabasco sauce

2 tablespoons dark rum

salt & freshly ground black pepper to taste

Mix all ingredients gently in a glass bowl.

Pan-Seared Sea Bass with Rum, Ginger & Vanilla Glaze

THE combination of rum, ginger, and vanilla makes a remarkable glaze for this fish. I like to serve it with celery hearts, the sweetest and most tender part of the celery.

makes 4 servings

1/4 cup dark rum

1/4 cup honey

1/4 cup lime juice

1/4 cup low-sodium soy sauce

3 tablespoons balsamic vinegar

1 tablespoon pure vanilla extract

1 tablespoon chopped fresh ginger

1 tablespoon minced fresh garlic

1 teaspoon cornstarch mixed with 1 tablespoon water

2 tablespoons extra-virgin olive oil

four 4- to 8-ounce sea bass fillets, skin-on

Preheat oven to 375°F.

In a saucepan, combine the rum, honey, lime juice, soy sauce, vinegar, vanilla, ginger, and garlic. Blend in the cornstarch mixture and cook until the sauce is thick enough to coat the back of a spoon.

In the meantime, in a sauté pan, heat the olive oil. Add the fish (skin side down) and sauté for 2 minutes. Transfer the fish to an ovenproof dish and pour the glaze on top.

Bake for 5 to 7 minutes, or until the fish is cooked to your liking.

Serve with celery hearts and julienne of salsify cooked slowly in butter until tender.

Left Bank "So Famous" Sesame-Seared Rare Tuna

FOR 21 years, people have come from miles around to taste this dish at The Left Bank. You MUST use very fresh tuna—bright red and literally transparent.

makes 4 servings

1³/₄ pounds sashimi-quality yellowfin tuna steak

1 cup white sesame seeds

2 tablespoons extra-virgin olive oil

1 cup julienne leeks

1 cup julienne green bell peppers

1 cup julienne red bell peppers

1 cup julienne yellow bell peppers

1 cup minced fresh mushrooms

¹/₂ cup low-sodium soy sauce

¹/₂ cup Beef or Chicken Stock (recipes on pages 238 and 240)

¹/₄ cup orange juice concentrate

wasabi and pickled ginger for garnish

Cut the tuna steak into large cubes, about 2 x 2 inches. Dip each cube of tuna into the sesame seeds, coating the fish entirely so that no tuna is visible.

In a nonstick frying pan, heat the olive oil and sear the tuna cubes on all four sides, only 1 minute for each side. The seeds should be golden brown and the tuna should remain rare. Set aside.

In the same frying pan, add the julienne vegetables and the mushrooms. Sauté for 2 minutes, or until tender. Add the soy sauce, stock, and orange juice concentrate.

Spoon the vegetables and sauce into the center of 4 dinner plates.

To prepare the tuna for serving, slice 4 of the cubes in half diagonally, from corner to corner. Cut the other 4 cubes into very thin slices. Arrange the tuna slices in a fan-shape around the vegetables on the plate.

Serve with prepared wasabi and pickled ginger.

incredible cuisine

Catfish with Lemon-Caper Sauce

THIS recipe is an easy introduction to cooking this delicate catfish, which is a mild-tasting fish with a great texture. No other fish quite compares to it! But if you prefer, you can replace it with snapper, mahi-mahi, or even swordfish.

makes 4 servings

four 6- to 8-ounce skinless and boneless catfish fillets

1 cup all-purpose flour, seasoned with salt & pepper, for dredging

1 tablespoon extra-virgin olive oil

$1/4$ cup finely diced red onions

$1/2$ cup dry vermouth

2 tablespoons freshly squeezed lemon juice

2 tablespoons small capers

1 teaspoon sugar in $1/4$ cup evaporated skim milk

Preheat oven to 375°F.

Dredge the fish fillets in the seasoned flour. Tap off the excess flour.

In a nonstick sauté pan, heat the olive oil to sizzling and sauté the catfish until a light golden brown on one side. Flip the fillets to the other side. Transfer to an ovenproof dish and bake in the preheated oven for 5 to 7 minutes, or until cooked to your liking.

In the meantime, in the same sauté pan, add the onions. Cook for 2 minutes until translucent. Add the vermouth and cook until reduced by half. Add the lemon juice, capers, and sweetened evaporated milk. Heat for less than 1 minute, but do not bring to a boil!

Take the fish out of the oven and arrange on serving plates with the sauce on top of each fillet.

Serve with couscous and asparagus spears gently sautéed in butter.

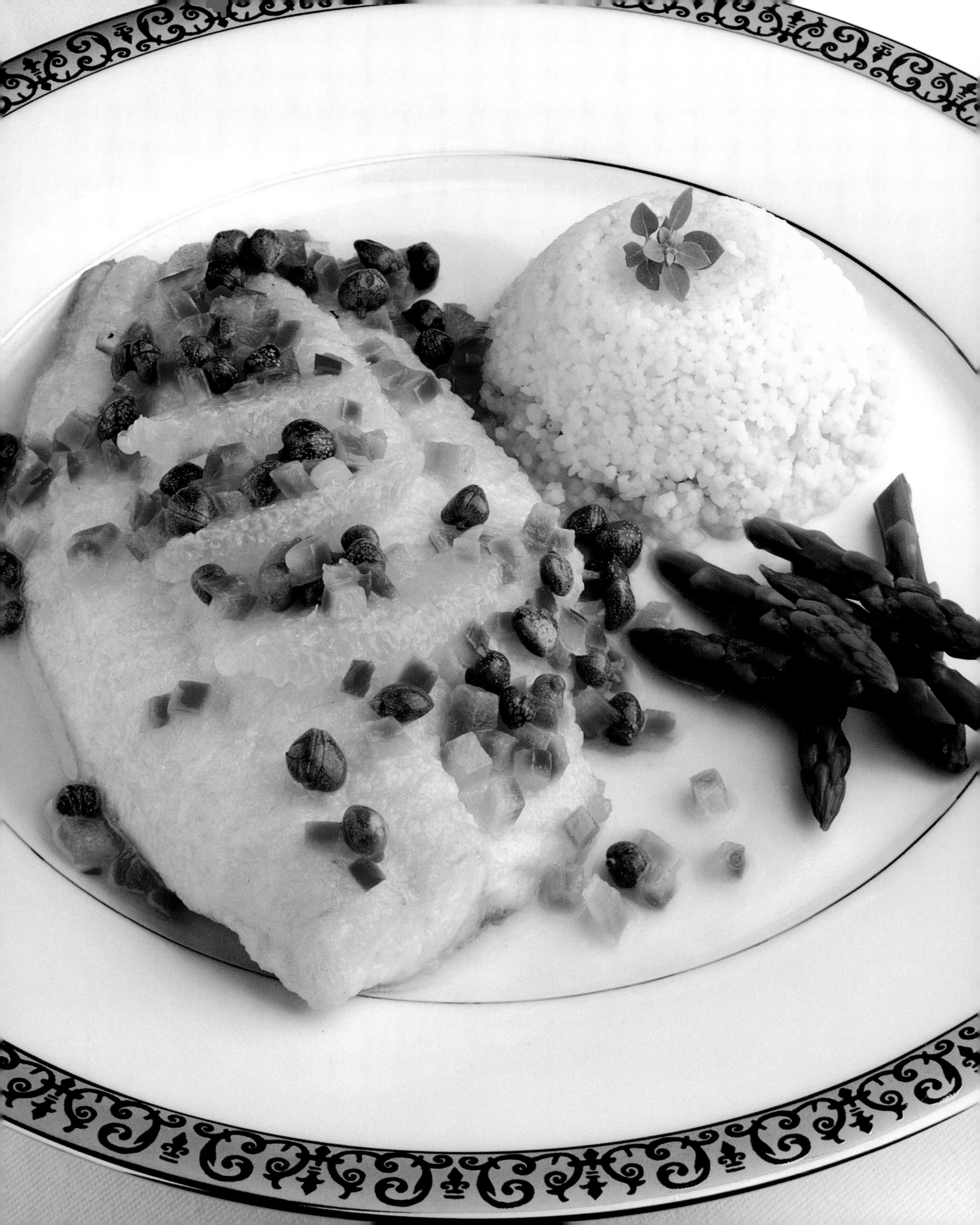

Blackened Sea Scallops
with Tomato-Curry Vinaigrette

DON'T let this list of ingredients scare you; it's only a bunch of spices. (If you're missing a few, don't worry about it.) The seasoning would also be great on chicken or another fish. As for the vinaigrette—let the blender do all the work!

makes 4 servings

20 sea scallops (25 to 30 count)

salt

Blackening Seasoning (recipe on page 132)

1 tablespoon extra-virgin olive oil

dill sprig for garnish

Season the scallops with salt and the Blackening Seasoning. In a nonstick sauté pan, heat the olive oil and when hot, sauté the scallops for 2 minutes on each side. Spoon the Tomato-Curry Vinaigrette onto serving plates and arrange the scallops on top.

tomato-curry vinaigrette

1 pound ripe tomatoes, peeled, seeded, and chopped, to make 1 cup

$^1/_2$ cup Chicken Stock (recipe on page 240)

1 tablespoon rice vinegar

3 tablespoons extra-virgin olive oil, divided

1 tablespoon chopped shallots

1 teaspoon chopped fresh garlic

1 tablespoon tomato purée

1 teaspoon curry powder

$^1/_2$ teaspoon chopped fresh ginger

$^1/_4$ teaspoon turmeric

$^1/_4$ teaspoon cumin

$^1/_4$ Anaheim pepper, cut into brunoise (tiny dice)

salt & freshly ground black pepper to taste

In a blender, combine the tomatoes, stock, rice vinegar, and 2 tablespoons of the olive oil. Blend for approximately 30 seconds and transfer to a bowl.

In a frying pan, heat the remaining 1 tablespoon olive oil and sauté the shallots until transparent. Add the garlic and when fragrant, add the tomato purée, curry, ginger, turmeric, cumin, and Anaheim pepper.

With a whisk, blend in the tomato mixture. Season with salt and pepper to taste. The vinaigrette can be made a day ahead. Serve at room temperature.

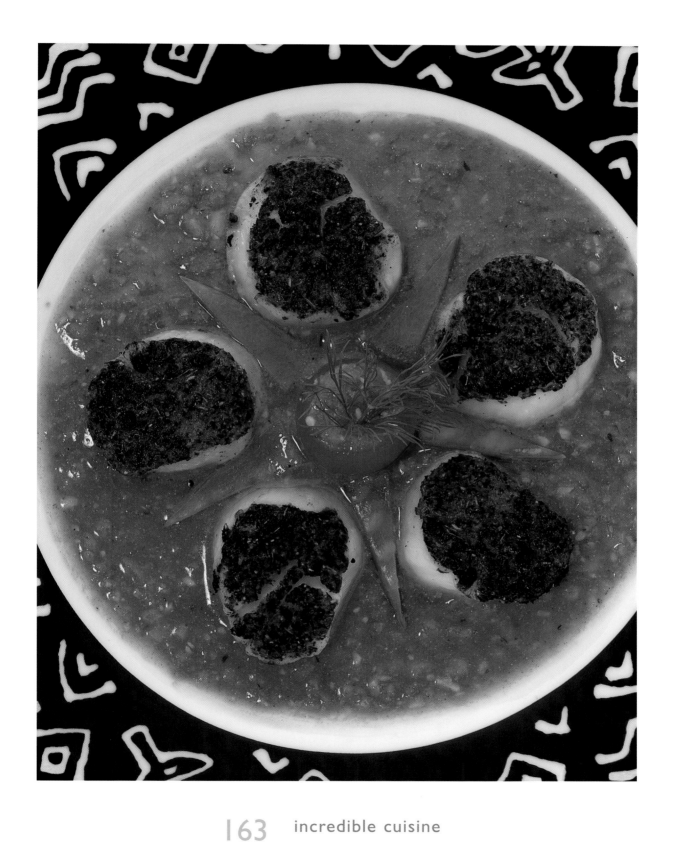

meats

When I first came to the United States, I was stunned by how often Americans ate meat, and by how much. My mother, being Italian, had always reserved meat for special events or for Sundays, when she would cook a leg of lamb or a nice-sized roast beef. So, somehow I still associate meat with special occasions. When I cook for close friends or family members, I will always prepare a meat entrée. I mean, what better way to show guests they're special than by serving something like the Roasted Filet Mignon with a Brandy & Peppercorn Sauce (page 176).

In selecting red meat, the single most important indicator of quality is marbling, which is fat. The marbling not only makes the meat very, very tender, it also makes it very tasty because the fat holds in the flavor. This may be one place where you don't want to skimp on fats! You will see heavy marbling throughout cuts marked "U.S. Prime," because it has the highest fat content. There will be somewhat less marbling in "U.S Choice," and almost no marbling at all in "U.S. Select." (Of course, the fat we are talking about is on the inside of the meat; there should be no more than $^3/_4$ inch of fat on the outside.) And meat should always be bright red in color when you buy it, not brown—or any other color, for that matter!

Pan-Seared Veal Chops
with Brandy Mustard Sauce

THIS recipe transforms a regular veal chop into something absolutely stunning, with a spectacular flavor. Yet ANYBODY can achieve this dramatic presentation at home—there is nothing, nothing to it! I like to serve this with the Wild Mushroom Risotto (recipe on page 104), but a barley and mushroom dish or a garlic mashed potato would also be fantastic.

makes 4 servings

2 tablespoons extra-virgin olive oil

4 very lean veal chops, 14 ounces each

salt & freshly ground black pepper to taste

1 cup chopped wild mushrooms (cremini, oyster, or shiitake)

2 shallots, minced

3/4 cup Beef or Chicken Stock (recipes on pages 238 and 240)

1/4 cup brandy

1 tablespoon tomato paste

1 tablespoon chopped fresh tarragon

1 tablespoon tarragon mustard

Preheat oven to 400°F.

In a sauté pan, heat the olive oil and, when hot, sear the veal chops on both sides until golden brown. Transfer to an ovenproof dish and bake for 15 minutes.

In the meantime, back to the same sauté pan, add the mushrooms, shallots, stock, brandy, tomato paste, and tarragon. Let reduce by half. Stir in the mustard and remove from the heat.

To serve, divide the sauce equally on serving plates and place a veal chop on each plate. To create the wonderful presentation as shown in the picture at right, I cut the meat from the bottom section of the chop, leaving the bone intact in the top half. The meat in the bottom half is then sliced and arranged in a fan-shape on the risotto. Place the top half of the chop behind the slices with the bone end standing up.

Sage & Shiitake Beef Tenderloin

HERE'S another easy-to-do presentation that looks very impressive. Just cut the tenderloin in half diagonally. Place one end standing up and cut the other side into as many slices as possible. Then fan them out on the plate, as shown. The sauce can be strained, or leave the mushrooms in—just as delicious.

makes 4 servings

2 tablespoons extra-virgin olive oil

four 6-ounce beef tenderloin steaks, all fat removed

2 tablespoons minced shallots

2 cups sliced shiitake mushrooms (or any other available mushrooms)

1 tablespoon minced fresh garlic

1 tablespoon minced fresh sage leaves

1 cup Cabernet Sauvignon or other full-bodied red wine

1 cup Beef Stock (recipe on page 238)

1 tablespoon cornstarch mixed with 2 tablespoons water

salt & freshly ground black pepper to taste

Preheat oven to 450°F.

In an ovenproof sauté pan, heat 1 tablespoon of the olive oil and when hot, add the tenderloin steaks. Sear on all sides until golden brown. Transfer the pan to the oven and cook for 6 to 8 minutes for medium rare.

In the meantime, make the sauce. In a saucepan, heat the remaining 1 tablespoon olive oil. Add the shallots and when they are golden brown, add the mushrooms. Sauté for 2 minutes. Add the garlic and sage. When they are both fragrant, pour in the wine and let reduce by half. Add the stock and cornstarch mixture. Let cook for 5 minutes. Adjust thickness with more cornstarch, if necessary. Adjust the seasoning with salt and pepper.

Spoon 2 to 3 tablespoons of sauce onto each of 4 dinner plates. Place a steak on top of the sauce.

Serve with Roasted Nouvelle Potatoes with Rosemary (recipe on page 199) and green beans.

Beef Carbonnade
(Beef Stew Cooked in Beer)

I learned this fantastic recipe from my grandmother on my father's side. She was from Belgium, and this was her favorite dish. She used a nice, dark, heavy beer, but it's just as good with a "lite" version. Like most stews, it reheats beautifully. It's a great, great meal.

makes 8 servings

1 tablespoon extra-virgin olive oil

2 pounds boneless chuck roast or top round, well-trimmed and cut into 2-inch cubes

1 slice 97% fat-free smoked ham, $1/4$ inch thick, cut into small cubes (approximately 4 ounces)

2 cups sliced yellow onions

1 tablespoon minced fresh garlic

3 cups Beef Stock (recipe on page 238)

$1^3/4$ pounds ripe tomatoes, peeled, seeded, and chopped, to make 2 cups

1 cup "lite" beer

$1/4$ cup tomato paste

2 tablespoons dark brown sugar

1 teaspoon fresh thyme leaves, minced

1 bay leaf

$1/4$ teaspoon salt

$1/2$ teaspoon freshly ground black pepper

In a large skillet or Dutch oven, heat the olive oil and add as many beef cubes as you can without crowding (if you crowd the skillet, the meat won't brown properly). Brown the cubes well on all sides. Remove each batch of browned beef from the skillet and set aside. Add the ham to the skillet on medium heat and cook until golden brown.

When the beef and ham have been browned, add the onions and cook, stirring occasionally, until golden brown. Add the garlic. When the garlic becomes fragrant (about 1 minute) add the stock, tomatoes, beer, tomato paste, brown sugar, thyme, and bay leaf.

Reduce heat to low and let simmer for $1^1/2$ to 2 hours, stirring occasionally, until the meat is very tender. After about an hour, check the consistency of the sauce. For a thicker stew, combine 1 tablespoon cornstarch and 2 tablespoons water, then add to the stew.

Adjust the seasoning with salt and pepper. Remove the bay leaf before serving.

Multigrain Cracker-Crusted Veal Scaloppine with Sautéed Spinach & Ham

THIS delicate and crunchy crust is made from good cracker crumbs flavored with dry herbs (which is the only use I have for dry herbs). The veal should be no more than $^1/_4$ inch thick, or the crust will burn before the veal is cooked.

makes 4 servings

eight 2- to 3-ounce veal scaloppine (top sirloin or loin)

$^1/_4$ teaspoon salt

$^1/_4$ teaspoon freshly ground black pepper

2 cups multigrain saltine cracker crumbs

$^1/_4$ teaspoon dried thyme leaves

$^1/_4$ teaspoon dried oregano

$^1/_4$ teaspoon dried rosemary

$^1/_4$ cup egg substitutes

1 tablespoon extra-virgin olive oil

Place the veal scaloppine between two pieces of clear plastic wrap or wax paper. Pound each to $^1/_4$ inch thick. Discard the wrap and season each scaloppine with salt and pepper on both sides.

Mix the cracker crumbs and dried spices. Dip each scaloppine in the egg and dredge in the seasoned crumbs.

In a sauté pan, heat the olive oil and sear each veal scaloppine until golden brown on both sides. Reduce heat and cook slowly until cooked to your liking.

sautéed spinach & ham

1 tablespoon extra-virgin olive oil

$^1/_2$ cup diced yellow onions

$^1/_4$ cup diced 97% fat-free smoked ham

3 cups spinach leaves, washed and dried

In a large saucepan, heat the olive oil, then add the onions and cook for 2 minutes until translucent. Add the ham and sauté for 2 minutes. Add the spinach and cook for 1 more minute, or until the spinach leaves are wilted. Serve immediately.

Blanquette de Veau
(Veal Stew with Onions & Mushrooms)

EVERY ingredient here is poached and remains white—hence, the name, which comes from the French word "blanc," meaning "white."

makes 8 servings

8 cups Chicken Stock (recipe on page 240)

1 whole onion, cut into large chunks, studded with 2 cloves

1 celery stalk, cut into 1-inch pieces

1 cup diced leeks

1 carrot, cut into $^1/_2$-inch pieces

$2^1/_4$ pounds lean breast of veal, cut into 2-inch cubes

12 very small new potatoes, peeled

24 pearl onions

24 very small button mushrooms (or regular size, quartered)

$^1/_2$ cup evaporated skim milk

1 tablespoon cornstarch mixed with 1 tablespoon water

salt & ground white pepper to taste

2 tablespoons chopped fresh parsley

In a large Dutch oven heat the stock. Add the onions, celery, leeks, carrots, and the bouquet garni.* Bring to a boil, reduce to low heat and add the meat. Let simmer on medium heat for approximately 1 hour, skimming any impurities that rise to the surface.

Remove the meat and the bouquet garni with a slotted spoon and set aside. Using an immersion blender, blend all the vegetables until very smooth. Strain through a fine sieve into a smaller saucepan. Add the meat, potatoes, onions, and mushrooms and cook for 45 additional minutes, or until the meat is very tender.

Add the evaporated milk and the cornstarch mixture. Season with salt and white pepper. Sprinkle with chopped parsley.

*Bouquet Garni (in cheesecloth)

2 sprigs fresh thyme

1 bay leaf

12 (about) parsley stems

12 (about) whole black peppercorns

Place all ingredients in cheesecloth and tie with string.

Veal Scaloppine with Baby Shrimp & Mushrooms

THIS classic was on the menu when The Left Bank opened, and it was my number one seller for 10 years. The original recipe had at least 4 ounces of garlic butter per person. Now you can enjoy the same flavor with minimal fat, thanks to my secret ingredient: Sun-Dried Tomato Pesto.

makes 4 servings

8 veal scaloppine, 3 ounces each

salt and freshly ground black pepper to taste

1 tablespoon extra-virgin olive oil

$^1/_4$ cup baby shrimp (60 to 70 count), peeled and deveined

$^1/_4$ pound fresh mushrooms, sliced

1 tablespoon minced fresh garlic

$^1/_2$ cup peeled, seeded, and chopped tomatoes

$^1/_4$ cup cream (sweet) sherry

2 tablespoons Sun-Dried Tomato Pesto (recipe on page 249)

Place each piece of veal between two pieces of clear plastic wrap or wax paper. Pound each one to $^1/_4$ inch thick. Discard the wrap and season the scaloppine on both sides with salt and pepper to your liking.

In a large nonstick sauté pan, heat the olive oil. When hot, add the veal and sauté for 2 to 3 minutes on each side until golden brown. Remove and set aside.

In the same sauté pan, add the baby shrimp and cook for 2 minutes. Add the mushrooms and cook for 2 to 3 additional minutes on medium heat. Add the garlic and, when fragrant (only 1 minute), add the tomatoes, sherry, and pesto. Cook for 3 to 4 minutes. Mix in the veal scaloppine and serve immediately.

Pot Roast with Nouvelle Potatoes & Cabernet Sauvignon Sauce

THIS is the finest pot roast I have ever eaten—and I have tasted many! After the meat cooks for 2 hours, slice it, return it to the sauce, and cook it for another 30 to 45 minutes. This creates a very moist and tender roast.

makes 6 servings

one 4-pound bottom round of beef

4 garlic cloves, split in half lengthwise

2 tablespoons extra-virgin olive oil, divided

1 onion, cut into 1-inch cubes

2 carrots, cut into 1-inch cubes

1 celery stalk, cut into 1-inch cubes

1 leek, cut into 1-inch cubes

2 cups Cabernet Sauvignon or other full-bodied red wine

$^1/_2$ cup tomato purée

2 cups Beef Stock (recipe on page 238)

2 bay leaves

2 sprigs fresh thyme

2 sprigs fresh rosemary

1 pound medium nouvelle potatoes, peeled

24 pearl onions (approximately)

2 tablespoons cornstarch, mixed with 2 tablespoons water (optional)

Trim excess fat from the meat. Secure loops of butcher's twine around the outside of the meat, every 1$^1/_2$ to 2 inches.

Using a very small paring knife, poke 2-inch-deep holes into the meat every 2 to 3 inches. Insert a clove of garlic in each hole (6 to 8 should be enough). In a heavy-bottom casserole, heat 1 tablespoon of the olive oil. Add the meat and brown on all sides, turning until a golden brown. Remove the meat and set aside.

To the casserole, add the onions, carrots, celery, and leeks. Sweat all the vegetables for 10 minutes. Place the meat on top of the vegetables, add the wine, tomato purée, stock, bay leaves, thyme, and rosemary. Cover and cook on very low heat for 2 hours.

Remove the meat and slice about $^1/_2$ inch thick. Strain and save the cooking juices, discard all the vegetables and return the juices and meat to the casserole.

In a separate sauté pan, heat the remaining 1 tablespoon olive oil, and sauté the potatoes and pearl onions until golden brown. Add them to the pot and cook with the pot roast for 30 minutes. Let the sauce reduce to the proper consistency. The sauce should coat the back of a spoon. If too thin, add the cornstarch mixture.

Roasted Filet Mignon with a Brandy & Peppercorn Sauce

THIS spicy peppercorn sauce is the perfect complement to the delicate filet mignon, whose flavor and tenderness make it the supreme cut of beef. Don't be afraid to use lots of pepper! You may also sneak in a little cream or a few dabs of butter to finish off the sauce.

makes 4 servings

4 beef filets mignons, 5 ounces each

1/4 teaspoon freshly cracked black peppercorns

1/4 teaspoon freshly cracked white peppercorns

2 tablespoons extra-virgin olive oil, divided

2 tablespoons finely chopped shallots

1/4 pound mixed mushrooms

2 tablespoons balsamic vinegar

1 1/2 cups Beef Stock (recipe on page 238)

1/4 cup brandy

1 tablespoon chopped fresh thyme leaves

1/2 cup evaporated skim milk

1 teaspoon cornstarch mixed with 1 tablespoon water

salt to taste

1 teaspoon green peppercorns

rosemary sprigs for garnish

Preheat oven to 450°F.

Roll the filets in the cracked peppercorns. In a roasting pan or ovenproof frying pan, heat 1 tablespoon of the olive oil and when hot, sear the filets on all sides until golden brown. Transfer the pan to the oven and roast for 7 to 8 minutes, turning the filets over after 3 to 4 minutes.

In the meantime, in a saucepan, heat the remaining 1 tablespoon olive oil and when hot, add the shallots. When golden brown, add the mushrooms and vinegar. Let reduce until almost dry. Add the stock, brandy, and thyme. Let it reduce by half. For a smoother texture, strain through a fine sieve. Add the evaporated milk and, just before it comes to a boil, add the cornstarch mixture. Adjust the seasoning with salt and the green peppercorns.

To serve, spoon 3 or 4 tablespoons of sauce on top of each filet. Garnish with rosemary sprig. Serve with Roger's Scalloped Potatoes (recipe on page 196).

Smoked Ham & Cream Cheese-Stuffed Pork Chops

THIS gives your pork chops a bit of glamour with very little effort.

makes 4 servings

8 ounces low-fat cream cheese, softened

1 teaspoon chopped fresh thyme

1 teaspoon chopped fresh oregano

4 center-cut pork chops, 10 to 12 ounces each

4 paper-thin slices 97% fat-free smoked ham

2 tablespoons extra-virgin olive oil, divided

2 shallots, chopped

1/4 pound mixed wild mushrooms

1/4 cup balsamic vinegar

1/2 cup Barolo or other full-bodied, Italian, red wine

1 cup Beef Stock (recipe on page 238)

1 tablespoon chopped fresh tarragon

salt & freshly ground black pepper to taste

fresh tarragon sprigs for garnish

Mix the cream cheese with the fresh herbs.

Preheat oven to 375°F.

Lay each chop flat on a cutting board. While holding down the meat with one hand, slice horizontally, from the meat side toward the bone, using the point of a knife to form a pocket. Cut deeply to the bone.

Wrap 2 ounces of cream cheese with one slice of ham, then stuff each chop. Press the meat together around the opening and secure with toothpicks, if necessary.

In an ovenproof sauté pan, heat 1 tablespoon of the olive oil and when hot, add the chops and cook for 3 to 4 minutes, until a golden brown. Turn chops over, transfer the pan to the oven, and bake for 10 minutes.

While the chops are cooking, start the sauce. In a saucepan, heat the remaining 1 tablespoon olive oil and when hot, add the shallots. Sweat the shallots for 2 minutes, then add the mushrooms and cook for 2 more minutes. Pour in the vinegar and let reduce until almost dry. Add the Barolo wine and let reduce by half. Add the stock. Reduce the sauce for 2 additional minutes. Stir in the chopped tarragon. Adjust the seasoning with salt and pepper.

Spoon some sauce onto each dinner plate and set a pork chop on top. Garnish with a sprig of fresh tarragon.

Pork Tenderloin & Garbanzo Bean Casserole

THIS wonderful pork stew calls for dry garbanzo beans; if you use canned, don't add them until the very end.

makes 4 servings

5 ounces dry garbanzo beans

6 cups Chicken Stock (recipe on page 240)

1 tablespoon extra-virgin olive oil

1¼ pounds pork tenderloin, cut into 1-inch cubes

1 cup pearl onions

3 cups cubed eggplant

1 cup baby carrots

2 tablespoons chopped fresh garlic

1 cup port wine

2 tablespoons chopped fresh thyme leaves

Soak the dry garbanzo beans overnight in 4 cups of water. Drain.

In a large kettle, bring the stock to a boil. Add the drained beans, cover, and let simmer for 30 minutes.

In the meantime, in a large Dutch oven, heat the olive oil, add the pork tenderloin, and sauté until golden brown on all sides. Remove the pork and set aside. Add the pearl onions to the same pan and when they are golden brown, add the eggplant and carrots. Sauté for 2 minutes. Add the garlic and when fragrant, add the sautéed pork, port wine, and thyme. Let reduce for 2 minutes. Add the beans and their liquid. Cover and let simmer for 1 more hour, or until the beans and pork are tender.

Citrus-Roasted Pork Tenderloin

YOU will love tasting that wonderful burst of citrus flavor with each bite of this pork. And few of my recipes are simpler to prepare, or quicker. Just be sure to leave enough time—at least 4 hours—for the pork to absorb the tangy marinade. Serve the pork with the Roasted-Garlic Mashed Potatoes (recipe on page 200). Mama mia, you won't believe how good it is!

makes 4 servings

4 garlic cloves, crushed

2 teaspoons grated orange zest

1 teaspoon grated lime zest

1 tablespoon chopped fresh rosemary

$1/2$ teaspoon freshly ground black pepper

2 pork tenderloins, 1 pound each, trimmed of fat

$1/3$ cup freshly squeezed orange juice

$1/4$ cup freshly squeezed lime juice

$1/4$ cup sherry

$1/4$ cup honey

2 tablespoons balsamic vinegar

1 tablespoon extra-virgin olive oil

In a small bowl, mash together the garlic, citrus zests, rosemary, and pepper. Rub onto the tenderloins.

Make a marinade of the orange juice, lime juice, sherry, honey, and vinegar. Set the tenderloins in a large glass container with the marinade. Cover and let it marinate in the refrigerator for at least 4 hours.

Preheat oven to 425°F.

Place a roasting pan on the stovetop and add 1 tablespoon olive oil. Sear the tenderloins on all sides until nicely browned. Drizzle 2 tablespoons of the marinade on the tenderloins. Roast in the oven for 5 to 7 minutes. Turn and baste with more marinade. Roast for an additional 5 minutes for a nice medium rare.

Place the tenderloins on a serving platter and slice into $1/4$-inch slices.

Pork Tenderloin with Red Beans & Jalapeño Relish

I happen to love ALL pork and beans together, but the unusual marriage of flavors, textures, and color in this dish is particularly stimulating. Try to cook your own beans, since canned beans lose their texture and lots of flavor. And oh, this jalapeño relish is outstanding! For a wonderful accompaniment, serve the Sweet Potato Mash (recipe on page 192). You will lick your plate clean!

makes 4 servings

2 pork tenderloins (about 2 pounds total weight), trimmed of fat

salt & freshly ground black pepper to taste

2 tablespoons extra-virgin olive oil, divided

$1/2$ cup minced onions

1 jalapeño chile pepper, finely diced

$1/2$ cup finely diced 97% fat-free smoked ham

1 tablespoon chopped fresh thyme leaves

1 cup Roasted Chicken Stock (recipe on page 239)

1 cup cooked pinto beans

2 tablespoons tomato purée

Preheat oven to 425°F.

Season the pork tenderloins with salt and pepper to your liking. In a large ovenproof sauté pan, heat 1 tablespoon of the olive oil and sauté the tenderloins until golden brown on all sides. Transfer the pan to the oven and roast the tenderloins for 7 to 8 minutes.

In the meantime, make the sauce. In a saucepan, heat the remaining 1 tablespoon olive oil and when hot, add the onions and jalapeños. When the onions become translucent, add the ham and thyme and sauté for 2 minutes. Add the stock, beans, and tomato purée. Cook for 10 minutes. Season with salt and pepper to taste.

Spoon some sauce onto each dinner plate. Slice the tenderloins into $1/4$-inch-thick slices and arrange attractively on the sauce.

Beef Stew "My Way"

STEWS were very big in the 1970s, and every Thursday we'd serve a Beef Bourguignon that was delicious, but intense in fat. Since then, this recipe has gotten lighter and lighter—and better and better! Not only does it taste incredible, but, trust me, it is also extremely simple to prepare.

makes 4 servings

1 tablespoon extra-virgin olive oil

2 pounds boneless chuck roast or top round, trimmed and cut into 2-inch cubes

20 pearl onions

6 paper-thin slices 97% fat-free smoked ham, cut into $1/4$-inch squares

1 tablespoon minced fresh garlic

1 cup Cabernet Sauvignon or other full-bodied red wine

5 cups Beef Stock (recipe on page 238)

20 baby carrots

$1^3/4$ pounds ripe tomatoes, peeled, seeded, and chopped, to make 2 cups OR one 28-ounce can recipe-ready tomatoes, drained

$1/4$ cup tomato purée

1 teaspoon minced fresh thyme

1 teaspoon minced fresh rosemary

1 bay leaf

$1/4$ teaspoon salt

$1/2$ teaspoon freshly ground black pepper

1 tablespoon cornstarch, mixed with 2 tablespoons water (optional)

In a large skillet or Dutch oven, heat the olive oil and add as many meat cubes as you can without crowding (if the skillet is too crowded, the meat won't brown properly). Brown the meat well on all sides, remove each batch as it browns, and set them aside. It may be necessary to add a little more olive oil.

When all of the beef has browned and been removed, add the onions to the skillet and cook, stirring occasionally, until they are golden brown. Add the ham and garlic and stir.

When the garlic is fragrant (about 1 minute), add the wine, the browned beef cubes plus their juices, stock, carrots, tomatoes, tomato purée, thyme, rosemary, and bay leaf.

Reduce heat to low, let simmer for $1^1/2$ to 2 hours, stirring occasionally, until the meat is very tender. After about an hour, check to see how liquid the stew seems; for a thicker stew, add the cornstarch mixture. Adjust the seasoning with salt and pepper and remove the bay leaf.

incredible cuisine

Roasted Pork Tenderloin with Balsamic, Honey & Vanilla Glaze

WHEN my old friend, cooking instructor Johnny Miller, demonstrated this recipe, my students raved. The sweet-and-sour balancing act between the balsamic vinegar and the honey and vanilla produces quite a taste sensation.

makes 4 servings

- 1 tablespoon extra-virgin olive oil
- 1 1/2 pounds center-cut pork tenderloin, trimmed of fat
- 2 tablespoons chopped shallots
- 1 tablespoon chopped fresh garlic
- 1/4 cup honey
- 1/4 cup balsamic vinegar
- 1 teaspoon chopped fresh oregano leaves
- 1 teaspoon pure vanilla extract

Preheat oven to 375°F.

Heat the olive oil in a sauté pan, add the pork tenderloin and pan sear the meat until golden brown on all sides. Remove the meat and set aside.

In the same pan with the meat drippings, add the shallots and sweat them for 2 minutes. Add the garlic and, when fragrant, stir in the honey and balsamic vinegar. Add the oregano and vanilla. Cook for 2 minutes at low heat.

Coat the seared pork tenderloin with the glaze. Place the pork on a rack in a roasting pan and roast for 10 to 12 minutes, or to your liking. Baste the pork periodically with the glaze.

Garlic Roasted Leg of Lamb
with Madeira Mushroom Sauce

A leg of lamb is one of the easiest cuts of meat to prepare. All you do is poke a few holes, stuff them with garlic, and rub the outside with herbs. Delicious! Serve it with Roasted Nouvelle Potatoes with Rosemary (recipe on page 199).

makes 4 servings

one 5- to 6-pound leg of lamb, all fat trimmed

12 small garlic cloves

3 tablespoons extra-virgin olive oil

1 tablespoon minced fresh rosemary

1 tablespoon minced fresh thyme

1 tablespoon minced fresh oregano

$1/4$ teaspoon salt

$1/4$ teaspoon freshly ground black pepper

Madeira Mushroom Sauce (recipe on page 243)

Preheat oven to 350°F.

Cut 12 slits into the lamb, about $1/2$ inch in length. Insert the garlic cloves into the slits.

In a small bowl, mix the olive oil, rosemary, thyme, oregano, salt, and pepper. Rub the oil mixture all over the lamb.

Roast the lamb for about 1 hour and 45 minutes for a nice medium rare. A meat thermometer should read 150°F.

While the lamb is roasting, make the sauce.

vegetables

I f I close my eyes, I can still see them: Mounds and mounds of fresh, colorful vegeta-bles—yellow and red and green and purple—piled high in the afternoon sun at the local market in the south of France. As a young boy, I would accompany my mother each day when she'd go to the market for her produce—smelling, feeling, and even weighing each piece to make sure it was ready to be eaten. She never had to coax me to eat my vegetables; they were so fresh and delicious, I couldn't resist them!

Nowadays, I think vegetables are often the most overlooked and least appreciated part of a meal. But vegetables round out a meal, add color and interest and texture to the plate. And, as your mother always told you, they're good for you, too.

I have included so many wonderful recipes for you in this book, I am sure you will find something to please even the most rabid vegetable-haters you know. Prepare the Sweet Potato Mash (page 192), and then get them to try just a bite. I know they'll be asking for more!

Sweet Potato Mash

DO me a favor: Please try this recipe! You have never tasted a sweet potato mash until you have had this one. The key to success is to mix the potatoes in a food processor for only a few seconds. If you overprocess, the texture will change and they will become rubbery. Also, you MUST use fresh rosemary with the corn—and be sure to chop it very fine.

1 1/2 pounds sweet potatoes, peeled, and chopped into 1-inch cubes

2 tablespoons pure maple syrup

1/4 teaspoon grated nutmeg

1/4 teaspoon ground cinnamon

1 tablespoon extra-virgin olive oil

1/2 cup diced onions

1 cup frozen corn kernels

1 tablespoon finely chopped fresh rosemary

salt & freshly ground black pepper to taste

Cook the potatoes in boiling water until tender. Combine in a food processor with the maple syrup, nutmeg, and cinnamon. Using the pulsing switch, mix enough to cream the potatoes. Do not over process.

In a sauté pan, heat the olive oil and add the onions. When translucent, add the corn and rosemary. Sauté for 3 to 4 minutes.

In a large serving bowl, mix the potatoes and corn. Adjust the seasoning with salt and pepper.

Baked Carrots

WHEN you want an interesting new way to serve a great old standby, try this baked carrot recipe. It makes an outstanding side dish. Just look at the ingredients—the flavor combination is fabulous! And if you do not have maple syrup in your pantry, try honey instead. It's a great substitute.

makes 6 servings

2 pounds carrots, peeled, and sliced $1/4$ inch on the bias

1 tablespoon extra-virgin olive oil

$1/2$ cup diced onions

1 tablespoon chopped fresh thyme leaves

$1/2$ cup Chicken Stock (recipe on page 240)

2 tablespoons pure maple syrup

1 tablespoon chopped fresh dill

Preheat oven to 375°F.

Poach the carrot slices in boiling water until slightly tender.

In a sauté pan, heat the olive oil and when hot, add the onions. When translucent, add the thyme. Cook for 2 minutes. Stir in the stock and maple syrup. Mix until smooth.

Add the cooked carrots and coat well. Sprinkle with the dill. Cover and bake for 10 minutes.

incredible cuisine

Mixed Vegetable Casserole

THIS is my version of a ratatouille, a great vegetable stew. If you like, add portobello mushrooms for extra texture. And, if you are missing a vegetable here or there, don't worry about it; as long as you don't forget the garlic, it will still be fine. This casserole can be served as a side dish or as a wonderful vegetarian main course, or it's great with pasta and some crusty bread.

makes 4 servings

1 teaspoon extra-virgin olive oil

¹/₄ cup minced white onions

¹/₄ pound button mushrooms, quartered

1 large carrot, sliced very thin or 12 baby carrots

1 red bell pepper, julienne

1 green bell pepper, julienne

2 tablespoons chopped fresh garlic

1 tablespoon chopped fresh thyme leaves

1 small zucchini, sliced ¹/₄ inch thick and slices cut in half

1 small yellow squash, sliced ¹/₄ inch thick and slices cut in half

1 very small eggplant, sliced ¹/₄ inch thick and slices cut in half

1 cup Chicken Stock (recipe on page 240)

1³/₄ pounds tomatoes, peeled, seeded, and diced, to make 2 cups OR one 28-ounce can recipe-ready tomatoes, drained

In a Dutch oven, heat the olive oil and when hot, add the onions. When translucent, add the mushrooms, carrots, and peppers. Sweat them for 2 minutes then add the garlic and thyme. When the garlic becomes fragrant, add the zucchini, yellow squash, and eggplant. Pour in the stock. Cover and cook for 15 minutes until all vegetables are tender. Add the tomatoes and cook for 5 more minutes.

White Bean & Smoked Ham Ragout

I really love to eat beans with almost anything. Cooked with smoked ham, beans are a great side dish for almost any pork or beef entrée, especially if the meat is barbecued. Besides tasting absolutely fantastic, this dish also happens to be very low in fat. I could eat it by the spoonful, right out of the pot. And as I'm cooking, I usually do!

makes 4 servings

12 ounces Great Northern beans

1 onion, quartered

1 celery stalk, cut into large chunks

3 garlic cloves

2 bay leaves

1 tablespoon extra-virgin olive oil

2 shallots, minced

$^{1}/_{4}$ cup diced 97% fat-free smoked ham

$^{1}/_{2}$ red bell pepper, cut into brunoise (tiny dice)

$^{1}/_{2}$ green bell pepper, cut into brunoise

2 tablespoons chopped fresh garlic

$1^{1}/_{2}$ cups Chicken Stock (recipe on page 240)

2 tablespoons chopped fresh parsley

Rinse the beans in cold water. Cover them with 4 times the amount of water and let them soak overnight.

The next day, drain off the water and place beans in a large soup kettle. Add 5 cups of water and bring to a boil. Add the onions, celery, garlic, and bay leaves. Lower the heat and cook the beans slowly, partially covered, for $1^{1}/_{2}$ hours, stirring often to avoid scorching. When the beans are tender—but not mushy—drain and discard the vegetables.

In a large saucepan, heat the olive oil and when hot, add the shallots, ham, and bell peppers. Sweat them for 2 minutes. Add the garlic and when fragrant, add the stock and the beans. Add the parsley and cook for 5 more minutes.

Roger's Scalloped Potatoes

ROGER, one of my sous-chefs at The Left Bank, has been working at the restaurant for almost 20 years. This is his favorite potato dish, and I'm certain it will soon become yours. These potatoes are fantastic! After you slice them, it is important to keep the peeled potatoes together until you are ready to place them on the cooking pan.

makes 4 servings

3 to 4 potatoes, peeled

salt & freshly ground black pepper to taste

2 large sprigs of fresh thyme

2 cups Chicken Stock (recipe on page 240)

$^{1}/_{2}$ cup (1 stick) butter, softened

Preheat oven to 425°F.

Thinly slice the potatoes, carefully making sure that you keep them together without separating, so that you can fan them easily into straight rows in the cooking pan. The slices should be no more than $^{1}/_{8}$ inch thick.

Spray a small lasagna pan or shallow casserole with non-stick cooking spray.

Arrange the potatoes in the pan with 2 sprigs of thyme. Add the stock, brush the tops with butter, and cover. Bake approximately 1 hour, or until the potatoes are tender.

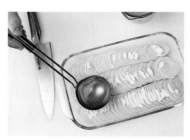

Roasted Shiitake & Cremini Mushroom Ragout

YOU can grill mushrooms, you can sauté them, but nothing is quite as gentle as roasting them in the oven.

makes 4 servings

1 1/2 pounds mixed shiitake and cremini mushrooms, sliced

2 shallots

2 garlic cloves

1/4 cup extra-virgin olive oil

4 sprigs fresh rosemary

4 sprigs fresh thyme

1 bay leaf

Preheat oven to 375°F.

In a glass bowl, mix all the ingredients. Transfer to a baking dish and cover with foil. Bake for 10 to 15 minutes, or until all the mushrooms are tender.

Roasted Nouvelle Potatoes with Rosemary

IS a meal without potatoes as unsatisfying to you as it is to me? I'm always looking for new ways to prepare—and eat!—potatoes. For this recipe, use nouvelle, or new, potatoes; regular white ones are too starchy for this dish. Also, be sure the potatoes are baked on low heat so they cook all the way through before the outside is too baked.

makes 4 servings

1 1/2 pounds small potatoes, scrubbed but not peeled

1/2 cup pearl onions

2 tablespoons extra-virgin olive oil

6 garlic cloves

4 sprigs fresh rosemary

2 tablespoons chopped fresh parsley

salt & freshly ground black pepper to taste

Preheat oven to 325°F.

Cut the potatoes into 1-inch cubes.

In an ovenproof dish, combine the potatoes, onions, olive oil, garlic, rosemary, salt, and pepper. Mix well. Cover and bake for 30 minutes, or until potatoes are tender all the way through.

Sprinkle with the parsley and serve immediately.

Roasted-Garlic Mashed Potatoes

THIS is one of my favorite mashed potato recipes in the world. The roasted garlic replaces the butter that would normally be used (of course, you could always add 3 to 4 ounces of butter for extra creaminess!). Roast the garlic long enough for it to become very soft and creamy, and make sure the milk is hot when you blend it with the garlic, or your potatoes will be lumpy.

makes 6 servings

1 large garlic head
1 tablespoon extra-virgin olive oil
2 sprigs fresh rosemary
freshly ground black pepper to taste
1$\frac{1}{2}$ pounds potatoes, peeled and quartered
$\frac{3}{4}$ cup milk
$\frac{1}{2}$ teaspoon baking soda
salt to taste

Preheat oven to 375°F.

Do not remove the papery outer skin from the garlic. With a very sharp knife, cut the garlic head in half horizontally. Set the halves side by side on a piece of foil, then drizzle with the olive oil. Arrange the sprigs of rosemary on each garlic half and sprinkle with pepper. Close the foil and roast for about 45 minutes, or until tender and buttery. The garlic will be mellow and easy to spread.

While the garlic is roasting, cook the potatoes in boiling, salted water until tender, approximately 30 minutes. Heat the milk.

Drain the potatoes and place in a large bowl. Mash the potatoes with a potato masher.

In a food processor, blend in the roasted garlic and hot milk until smooth and creamy. Combine the garlic and milk mixture with the potatoes. Add salt and pepper to taste.

Goat Cheese Polenta

POLENTA is a ground cornmeal that is cooked in broth. When I was very young, I'm sure that I ate as much polenta as I did potatoes. And now, little by little, it is becoming more popular here in America. It may take a little time to create a fluffy and creamy polenta, but I know you will come to love it as much as your favorite mashed potatoes.

makes 4 servings

2 cups Chicken Stock (recipe on page 240)

1¹/₂ cups water

1 cup coarsely ground cornmeal

salt & ground white pepper to taste

¹/₂ cup low-fat sour cream

¹/₄ cup crumbled goat cheese

In a large saucepan (preferably nonstick), combine the stock, water, and cornmeal over medium heat. Using a wooden spoon, mix until it comes to a boil. Immediately reduce the heat and keep mixing, scraping the sides and bottom, to avoid sticking or burning. Continue stirring for 30 minutes. Remove from the heat and let it cool for 10 minutes.

Season with salt and white pepper. Add the sour cream and goat cheese.

Serve immediately as a soft polenta. Or you may wish to make it in advance and reheat it later. Pour it into a lasagna pan and let it cool until firm. You can then slice it and reheat it on the grill or under the broiler.

Sweet Potatoes, Pearl Onions & Raisins with Honey & Balsamic Vinegar Glaze

THIS is a festive and lovely dish for the holidays.

makes 8 servings

1 cup raisins marinated in 1¼ cups port wine

2 cups pearl onions

½ cup honey

½ cup Chicken Stock (recipe on page 240)

3 tablespoons balsamic vinegar

1 tablespoon pure vanilla extract

3 to 4 large sweet potatoes, cut in half lengthwise

Marinate the raisins in the port wine for at least 4 hours at room temperature (better yet, overnight).

Preheat oven to 400°F.

Mix the marinated raisins, onions, honey, stock, vinegar, and vanilla.

Poach the potatoes until they are tender but not mushy. Transfer the poached potatoes to an ovenproof baking dish. Pour the onion-raisin mixture over the potatoes, cover, and bake for 10 minutes. Stir and bake for 10 additional minutes.

Braised Endive & Wild Mushrooms

GROWING up, I ate endive all the time, and my mom often used this recipe. The port wine is the perfect offset to the endive's slight bitterness.

makes 4 servings

4 to 6 Belgian endive

salt & freshly ground black pepper to taste

$1/4$ pound wild mushrooms, cleaned (but not sliced)

$1/2$ cup pearl onions

5 to 6 garlic cloves

2 cups Chicken Stock (recipe on page 240)

$1/2$ cup port wine

3 sprigs fresh thyme

$1/2$ cup freshly grated Reggiano Parmesan cheese

Preheat oven to 350°F.

Remove any discolored outer leaves from the endive. Cut endive in half lengthwise and sprinkle with salt and pepper (try to open the leaves without breaking them apart).

In an ovenproof dish, arrange endive halves side by side. Add the mushrooms, pearl onions, and garlic. Add the stock, port wine, and thyme. Cover with foil and bake for $1^{1}/_{2}$ hours, or until tender.

Raise the oven temperature to 500°F. Uncover the dish. Sprinkle with the Parmesan cheese. Continue to bake, uncovered, for 15 minutes.

Diced Potatoes & Onions

THIS is the perfect little recipe for a satisfying side dish. It's a great complement to so many main courses, ranging from an omelette to a fancy filet mignon. And it takes only 5 minutes to cook. Make sure you watch the ham and potatoes carefully—the smaller the cubes, the faster they will cook.

makes 4 servings

1 pound large red potatoes, peeled, rinsed, and dried

1 tablespoon extra-virgin olive oil

$^1/_2$ cup diced onions

1 cup diced 97% fat-free smoked ham

1 tablespoon chopped fresh garlic

2 tablespoons chopped fresh parsley

$^1/_4$ teaspoon salt

$^1/_4$ teaspoon freshly ground black pepper

Cut the potatoes into $^1/_2$-inch cubes.

In a heavy skillet, heat the olive oil then add the onions. When they become translucent, add the potatoes and ham. Cook over medium heat until the potatoes are tender in the center.

Add the garlic and continue to cook for 2 to 3 additional minutes. Keep checking the pan and moving it around to avoid overcooking the garlic.

Sprinkle with the parsley. Adjust the seasoning with salt and pepper. Serve immediately.

desserts

Making dessert is very, very different from every other form of cooking. It's really more like chemistry. That's because it's a precise science: You must follow the dessert recipes to the absolute letter, because the proportions are measured out to interact with one another in a certain way. With other forms of cooking, there's more room for creativity, for adjusting the quantity of certain ingredients—or even leaving some out altogether. You can't do that with desserts. If you change the amount of just one thing, you risk ruining the dish.

But this doesn't mean you should be afraid of making desserts. On the contrary: You are absolutely guaranteed good results with these recipes, as long as you follow the directions. Granted, you must take the time to read each one through a few times, to be sure you really understand the mechanics: Which step is done when? Do you have all the ingredients on hand? How many bowls will you need? What kinds of equipment?

I recommend you start with the Black Cherry Clafoutis (page 218), a delicious custard pie that is one of my all-time favorite desserts; it is impossible to mess up!

Low-Fat Chocolate & Orange Torte

CHOCOLATE and orange—now that's a match made in heaven! This torte is just out of this world. And the best part is, it's so low in fat. But don't tell your guests until after they've had a second slice. The Mango Coulis (recipe on page 253) is the perfect accompaniment.

makes 16 servings

2 cups low-fat milk

1 cup sugar, divided

3 cups unsweetened cocoa powder

8 egg substitutes

2 tablespoons pure vanilla extract

1 cup Curaçao, Grand Marnier, or other orange liqueur

1 tablespoon orange extract

1 tablespoon grated orange zest

3 packages unflavored gelatin

5 egg whites

Spray a 9-inch springform pan with nonstick cooking spray. In a saucepan, heat the milk with $^1/_2$ cup of the sugar. Add the cocoa powder and mix well until dissolved. Whisk in the egg substitutes and mix well until the first few heat bubbles start to surface. Stir in the vanilla.

In another saucepan, combine the orange liqueur, orange extract, orange zest, and the gelatin. Bring to a boil and mix well. Combine with the milk mixture and transfer to a glass or stainless steel bowl. Refrigerate for 2 hours.

In a separate bowl, use an electric mixer with clean, dry beaters to beat the egg whites. Start at low speed and increase the speed as peaks form. Slowly add the remaining $^1/_2$ cup sugar. Fold the egg whites gently into the chocolate filling with a spatula. Do not overmix the filling. Pour the mixture into the prepared pan.

Refrigerate for at least 2 to 3 hours or, for even better results, leave in the freezer overnight.

Vanilla, Chocolate & Kahlúa Chiffon Cake with Port Wine & Raspberry Sauce

SOMETIMES I go on a very strict nonfat diet to lose the extra pounds that slowly creep up from good living. But then my craving for sweets gets even stronger. So, when I make this recipe, I use 1 cup of applesauce instead of the $^1/_2$ cup of oil.

makes 16 servings

2 cups sifted cake flour

1$^1/_2$ cups sugar, divided

3 tablespoons unsweetened cocoa powder

1 teaspoon baking powder

1 teaspoon baking soda

$^1/_4$ teaspoon salt

$^1/_2$ cup sunflower oil

2 tablespoons Kahlúa or other coffee-flavored liqueur

2 tablespoons pure vanilla extract

7 large egg whites

1 teaspoon cream of tartar

nonstick cooking spray or oil to brush on baking pan

Port Wine & Raspberry Sauce (recipe on page 255)

Preheat oven to 325°F.

Into a large mixing bowl, sift together the flour, 1 cup of the sugar, the cocoa powder, baking powder, baking soda, and salt. Make a well in the center and add the oil, Kahlúa and vanilla. Do not mix.

In another bowl, beat the egg whites and cream of tartar until white and foamy. Slowly add the remaining $^1/_2$ cup sugar and continue beating until stiff peaks form. Do not overbeat. Mix $^1/_4$ of the egg whites until well incorporated into the flour mixture. Gently fold in the remaining egg whites using a rubber spatula.

Spray a 9-inch tube pan with nonstick cooking spray, or brush the inside with oil. Dust with flour and tap out the excess. Pour the batter into the prepared pan. Bang the mold on the counter to remove any air bubbles.

Bake for 55 minutes, or until the top feels springy, or until a cake tester inserted into the center comes out clean. Cool the cake upright on a wire rack for 1 hour. Loosen the sides with a small, thin knife. Remove the cake from the pan and allow it to cool. Wrap airtight, or serve immediately with a light sifting of confectioners' sugar accompanied by the Port Wine & Raspberry Sauce.

Lemon Chiffon Cake
with Apricot & Orange Coulis

I'VE tasted many chiffon cakes in my day, but never one so fluffy and flavorful. I like it in the morning with apricot jam or for dessert with a great coulis. And, like the Vanilla & Chocolate Chiffon Cake, if you want to make this one low-fat, just substitute the oil with 1 cup of applesauce.

makes 18 servings

2 cups sifted cake flour

1 1/2 cups sugar, divided

1 teaspoon baking powder

1 teaspoon baking soda

pinch salt

1/2 cup sunflower oil

1 tablespoon grated lemon zest (approximately 2 lemons)

1/4 cup freshly squeezed lemon juice

2 tablespoons pure vanilla extract

7 large egg whites

1 teaspoon cream of tartar

nonstick cooking spray or oil to brush on baking pan

Apricot & Orange Coulis (recipe on page 254)

Preheat oven to 325°F.

Into a large mixing bowl, sift together the flour, 1 cup of the sugar, baking powder, baking soda, and salt. Make a well in the center and add the oil, lemon zest, lemon juice, and vanilla. Do not mix.

In a bowl of an electric mixer, beat the egg whites and cream of tartar until white and foamy. Slowly add the remaining 1/2 cup sugar and continue beating until stiff peaks form. Do not overbeat. Mix 1/4 of the egg whites until well incorporated into the flour mixture. Gently fold in the remaining egg whites using a rubber spatula.

Spray a 9-inch tube pan with nonstick cooking spray, or brush the inside with oil. Dust with flour and tap out the excess. Pour the batter into the prepared pan. Bang the mold on the counter to remove any air bubbles.

Bake for 55 minutes, or until the top feels springy, or until a cake tester inserted into the center comes out clean. Cool the cake upright on a wire rack for 1 hour. Loosen the sides with a small, thin knife. Remove the cake from the pan and allow it to cool. Wrap airtight, or serve immediately with a light sifting of confectioners' sugar along with the Apricot & Orange Coulis.

Vanilla & Raspberry Crème Brûlée

DESSERT seems to be the one time when people don't want to worry about fat and calories. If you're going to indulge, make it with a fabulous treat like this!

makes 6 servings

6 egg yolks
$1/2$ cup sugar
2 cups heavy cream
2 tablespoons pure vanilla extract
1 pint fresh raspberries, or frozen
6 tablespoons sugar to caramelize the tops

Whisk together the egg yolks and sugar until thick and pale. The consistency should be that of a mousse.

Heat the cream in a stainless steel saucepan over medium heat and stir in the vanilla. Remove from the heat just before the boiling point.

Whisking all the while, slowly pour the hot cream into the egg yolks until well combined. Whisking keeps the egg yolks from scrambling. Strain the mixture through a sieve into a saucepan and return to medium-low heat and stir constantly until the mixture is thick enough to coat the back of a spoon. (To test, dip a spoon into the custard, turn it over and run your finger down the back of the spoon. If it leaves a clear path, the custard is done.)

Sprinkle about a dozen raspberries into each of 4 heat-proof custard dishes. Pour the custard over the berries and refrigerate for at least 6 hours.

To serve, sprinkle about 1 tablespoon sugar over the top of each custard and place under the broiler for about 3 minutes, until the sugar caramelizes (melts and turns light brown). You don't want the custard to get too warm. If you have a propane torch, use it to caramelize the sugar on each custard. Serve immediately.

Chocolate & Banana Crème Brûlée

IN France they would say that a true crème brûlée would not include fruit. But I say, hey! We're in America; we do what we want to do here! And in my opinion, this dessert is an excellent variation on the classic theme.

makes 6 servings

2 cups heavy cream, divided

2 tablespoons pure vanilla extract

8 ounces semisweet chocolate, chopped

6 egg yolks

2 bananas

6 tablespoons sugar to caramelize the tops

Preheat oven to 350°F.

In a saucepan, heat 1³/₄ cups of the cream and the vanilla. Bring to a boil. Add the chocolate and mix well.

In a separate bowl, lightly whisk the egg yolks and the remaining ¹/₄ cup of cream. Add the hot cream mixture slowly. Mix well.

Slice the bananas and divide equally on the bottom of 6 heatproof custard dishes. Pour the cream mixture on top of the bananas.

Bake in a bain-marie* for 35 minutes.

To serve, sprinkle about 1 tablespoon of sugar over the top of each custard and place under the broiler for about 3 minutes, until the sugar caramelizes (melts and turns light brown). You don't want the custard to get too warm. If you have a propane torch, use it to caramelize the sugar on each custard. Serve immediately.

*Bain-marie (water bath): Place the filled dishes in a large, shallow pan of hot water (dishes should sit three-quarters in the water). The water surrounds the crème brûlée with gentle heat, which protects the delicate custard from curdling.

banana!

Caramel Custard with a Strawberry & Raspberry Sauce

MAKING caramel may be a little tricky for you the first time you try. But as you do it, you will see that it's not complicated. If you keep an eye on it so that it does not turn too dark, it will be perfect.

makes 8 servings

1 cup sugar
1 1/4 cups water, divided

In a saucepan, heat the sugar and 1 cup water on high heat. The sugar will start to turn a golden brown in approximately 10 minutes; be careful, because it will burn very quickly. As soon as it turns a dark golden brown, turn off the heat and add the remaining 1/4 cup of water. Pour into 8 individual 6-ounce heatproof custard cups. Tilt the custard cups so that the caramel evenly covers the bottom and all sides. Let it cool in the refrigerator until it is ready.

the custard

6 eggs
3/4 cup sugar
3 cups hot milk
2 tablespoons pure vanilla extract

Preheat oven to 350°F.

In a large glass bowl, beat the eggs and add the sugar slowly while still beating. When the mixture is light and foamy, add the hot milk in a steady and thin stream. Add the vanilla and blend well. Pour into the prepared custard cups.

Set the custard cups in a hot water bath, up to 3/4 inch from the top rim of the cups. Bake for 45 minutes or until the tip of a small knife inserted in the custard comes out clean. Refrigerate for at least 4 to 5 hours.

To unmold, run a small, thin knife around the inside of each custard cup to loosen the custard. Turn a serving plate upside down over each custard cup, check to see if each one has loosened, then invert the plate. Serve with the Strawberry & Raspberry Sauce (recipe below).

strawberry & raspberry sauce

1 pint mixed berries
1/4 cup orange juice
1/4 cup sugar
2 tablespoons Curaçao, Grand Marnier, or other orange liqueur

Blend all the ingredients in your food processor or blender, strain through a fine sieve, and serve.

Black Cherry Clafoutis (Custard Pie)

I can still remember my mother preparing this dessert, which is probably one of my all-time favorites. It is also one of the easiest possible desserts in the world. You aren't supposed to cut the clafoutis until it cools—but I can never hold out that long!

makes 10 servings

1 cup all-purpose flour
$\frac{1}{2}$ cup sugar
$\frac{1}{8}$ teaspoon salt
4 eggs
1 cup milk
1 cup heavy cream
1 tablespoon pure vanilla extract
nonstick cooking spray
3 cups sweet black cherries, pitted, and well drained (if canned, drain very well)
2 tablespoons confectioners' sugar

Preheat oven to 350°F.

In a blender, combine the flour, sugar, salt, eggs, milk, cream, and vanilla. Blend thoroughly.

Generously spray the bottom of a 9-inch glass or ceramic baking dish with the nonstick cooking spray. Spread the cherries evenly on the bottom of the baking dish. Pour the batter slowly over the fruit.

Place the dish on the center oven rack and bake for 50 minutes until puffy and golden in color. Remove from the oven and dust with confectioners' sugar.

Cool before serving. Serve cold, or at room temperature.

Cinnamon Crêpes Stuffed with Chocolate Ice Cream & Bananas

TALK about versatile—crêpes are perfect for breakfast OR dessert. Prepare the batter a day before you want to use it, to make the crêpes less starchy. The rest is up to you: Stuff them with anything you like, or eat them plain with a little confectioners' sugar.

makes 4 servings

1 cup all-purpose flour
1/4 cup sugar
1 cup milk
2 eggs
1 tablespoon sunflower oil
1/4 teaspoon ground cinnamon
chocolate ice cream
4 bananas
confectioners' sugar for dusting

Place the flour, sugar, milk, eggs, oil, and cinnamon in a bowl and whisk until very smooth. Strain through a fine sieve, cover, and refrigerate for at least 3 hours, preferably overnight.

Heat a 6-inch nonstick crêpe or omelet pan and grease with a tiny amount of butter. Pour in about 2 tablespoons of batter and tip the pan to spread the batter evenly to produce a thin, delicate crêpe.

Cook the crêpe over medium heat until the bottom is lightly browned, then turn it over and brown the other side lightly. Transfer to a plate and repeat. Stack the crêpes with parchment or wax paper between them to prevent sticking. Wrap the stack and refrigerate until ready to use.

The crêpes may be made 1 day ahead.

Stuff each refrigerated crêpe with your favorite chocolate ice cream and sliced bananas. Roll up each one, sprinkle with confectioners' sugar, and serve immediately.

Kahlúa & Chocolate Flan

THIS is a delicious, custardy flan, and it is so, so easy to do. It's the perfect recipe to use when you need a special dessert that you can make ahead. I usually keep some in my refrigerator all the time—for as long as it lasts, that is. It's hard to resist eating this one by the spoonful right out of the mold!

makes 4 servings

3 cups milk

4 eggs

1/2 cup sugar

3 tablespoons unsweetened cocoa powder

3 tablespoons instant coffee granules

2 tablespoons pure vanilla extract

2 tablespoons Kahlúa or other coffee-flavored liqueur

Preheat oven to 325°F.

In a saucepan, heat the milk to a boiling point then remove it from the heat.

In a bowl, whisk the eggs, sugar, cocoa, coffee granules, vanilla, and Kahlúa. Add 2 to 3 tablespoons of the hot milk to temper the eggs (this will prevent scrambling the eggs). Then slowly add all the milk while you are constantly mixing. Strain through a fine sieve. Pour into 6- to 8-ounce custard molds.

Bake in a bain-marie (see page 216) for 45 minutes. Cool for at least 3 hours.

Cappuccino Mousse Pie

THIS magnificent recipe is best when served very, very cold—right out of the refrigerator or freezer.

makes 10 servings

4 ounces vanilla wafers
1 teaspoon water, if necessary
$^1/_4$ cup walnuts

To make the crust, place the wafers in a food processor with a metal blade and process until finely crushed.

Add the nuts until chopped into small pieces. Add a few drops of water, if necessary, to bind the ingredients. Press the mixture evenly and firmly onto the bottom of a 9-inch or 10-inch springform pan. Refrigerate the crust while you make the filling.

the pie filling

2 cups sugar, divided
$1^1/_3$ cups unsweetened cocoa powder
3 heaping tablespoons instant coffee (French roast) granules
$1^1/_2$ cups 2% milk
1 cup Kahlúa or other coffee-flavored liqueur
4 envelopes gelatin
$^1/_2$ cup water
16 ounces low-fat vanilla yogurt
2 tablespoons pure vanilla extract
4 egg whites

In a medium saucepan, mix $1^1/_2$ cups of the sugar, the cocoa, and coffee. Gradually whisk in enough milk to form a smooth paste. Working over medium heat, add the remaining milk and the coffee liqueur, stirring constantly with a wooden spoon. Let simmer for 2 minutes.

In a separate bowl, dilute the gelatin in water and let it soften for 5 minutes. Add the hot milk mixture to the gelatin and let it cool using an ice bath, or simply by placing it in the refrigerator for 2 hours. When the mixture is cold enough to have a thick texture (like whipped cream), add the yogurt and the vanilla.

In another bowl, use an electric mixer with clean, dry beaters to beat the egg whites. Start at low speed and increase the speed as peaks form. Slowly add the remaining $^1/_2$ cup sugar. When the whites are stiff but not dry, fold them gently into the cappuccino filling.

Do not overmix. Pour the batter into the prepared pan with the crust and refrigerate for at least 12 hours.

If you like, serve with the Port Wine & Raspberry Sauce (recipe on page 255).

Chocolate Kahlúa Cake

THIS has the same texture and flavor as the richest chocolate mousse you've ever tasted.

makes 10 servings

4 ounces chocolate wafers
2 ounces chopped almonds
1 teaspoon water, if necessary

To make the crust, place the wafers in a food processor fitted with a metal blade. Process until finely crushed. Add the almonds until chopped into about $1/8$-inch pieces. Add a few drops of water, if necessary. Press the mixture evenly and firmly onto the bottom of a 10-inch springform pan (see note below). Refrigerate the crust and make the cake filling.

Pour the cake filling into the prepared pan with the crust and bake for $1\frac{1}{2}$ hours. Turn off heat, and let it remain in the oven with the door open for 1 hour. Refrigerate the cake for at least 12 hours or, better, freeze overnight.

Note: If your springform pan has lost some of its spring, cover the bottom and halfway up the sides with foil to prevent any leaking batter from landing on the bottom of your oven and burning.

the cake filling

8 ounces dried apricots
$1/4$ cup cognac
4 egg substitutes
$1\frac{1}{2}$ cups sugar, divided
24 ounces low-fat sour cream
8 ounces low-fat vanilla yogurt
$1/4$ cup Kahlúa or other coffee flavored liqueur
2 tablespoons pure vanilla extract
$3/4$ cup self-rising flour
$1/4$ cup unsweetened cocoa powder
1 teaspoon baking powder
4 egg whites

Chop the apricots into $1/4$-inch cubes. In a saucepan, bring the cognac to a boil and add the apricots. Remove from the heat and let stand until cool.

Preheat oven to 350°F.

Use an electric mixer to beat the egg substitutes and 1 cup of the sugar. Beat at high speed for 5 minutes until pale yellow. On low speed, add the sour cream, yogurt, Kahlúa, and vanilla. Beat 3 to 4 more minutes. In a separate bowl, mix the flour, cocoa, and baking powder. Add to the mixer slowly until all the ingredients are incorporated. Add the apricot mixture and mix 2 more minutes.

In a separate bowl, use an electric mixer with clean, dry beaters to beat the egg whites; start at low speed and increase the speed as peaks form. Slowly add the remaining $1/2$ cup of sugar. When the whites are stiff but not dry, fold them gently into the Kahlúa mixture with a spatula. Do not overmix the filling.

Low-Fat Pumpkin Cheesecake

A year after I prepared this cake on the Today Show, I was still receiving requests for the recipe. Try to make it the day before so it can thicken to the proper consistency.

makes 16 slices

1 cup cooked couscous (couscous cooking directions on page 136)

2 tablespoons confectioners' sugar

1 tablespoon unsweetened cocoa powder

24 ounces low-fat cream cheese, softened

6 ounces low-fat sour cream

4 egg yolks

1 cup sugar, divided

8 ounces canned pumpkin

2 tablespoons pure vanilla extract

1 teaspoon orange extract

4 egg whites

To make the crust, place the couscous in a food processor fitted with the metal blade and process until finely crushed. Add the confectioners' sugar and cocoa powder and, while the blade is turning, add a few drops of water. Press the mixture evenly and firmly onto the bottom of a springform pan, making a fist and using the back of your hand and fingers. Refrigerate the crust while you make the filling.

Preheat oven to 325°F.

Use an electric mixer to beat the cream cheese until smooth. On low speed, add the sour cream. Add the egg yolks, $1/2$ cup of the sugar, the pumpkin, and the vanilla and orange extracts.

In a separate bowl, use an electric mixer with clean, dry beaters to beat the egg whites; start at low speed and increase the speed as peaks form. Slowly add the remaining $1/2$ cup of sugar. When the whites are stiff but not dry, gently fold them in the cream cheese-and-pumpkin mixture.

Pour the batter into the pan with the prepared crust. Bake approximately 1 hour, until the cake has risen and browned slightly and it just shimmies when you gently move the pan. It's a good idea to place the springform on a low, flat pan such as a pizza pan, to catch any batter that leaks. Turn the heat off and let the cake stand in the oven for 1 more hour. Remove the cake from the oven and let it cool at least 6 hours before serving. You can make this cake a couple of days ahead.

Raspberry & Vanilla Cheesecake

THIS wonderful cheesecake is the number one dessert at The Left Bank.

makes 16 slices

6 ounces chocolate wafers

24 ounces cream cheese, softened

8 ounces sour cream

2 tablespoons pure vanilla extract

8 eggs

1 1/2 cups sugar, divided

1/4 cup raspberry purée (see note below)

4 egg whites

Note: To make raspberry purée, take 1 pint of fresh or frozen raspberries, process very fine in a food processor, and strain through a very fine sieve.

To make the crust, place the wafers in a food processor fitted with the metal blade and process until finely crushed. Add a couple drops of water. Press the mixture evenly and firmly onto the bottom of a springform pan (see note below), making a fist and using the back of your hand and fingers. Refrigerate the crust while you make the filling.

Preheat oven to 325°F.

Using an electric mixer with the paddle attachment, beat the cream cheese until smooth. On low speed, add the sour cream and vanilla and set aside. In a clean mixing bowl, using the whisk attachment, combine the eggs and 1 cup of the sugar. Whisk for 4 to 5 minutes until fluffy. Fold in the softened cream cheese mixture. Separate this mixture into two large glass bowls. To one of the bowls, add the raspberry purée, mix well.

In another bowl, using an electric mixer with clean, dry beaters, beat the egg whites. Start at low speed and increase the speed as peaks form. Slowly add the remaining 1/2 cup of sugar. When the whites are stiff but not dry, scrape them equally into the two bowls of filling and use a spatula to gently fold them in. Don't overmix the filling.

Pour alternating plain mixture and raspberry mixture into the prepared pan until the pan is filled. Bake for approximately 1 hour, until the cake has risen and browned slightly and it just shimmies when you gently move the pan. It's a good idea to place the springform on a low, flat pan, such as a pizza pan, to catch any batter that leaks. Turn the heat off and let the cake stand in the oven for 1 more hour. Remove the cake from the oven and cool before serving. You can make this cake a day ahead.

Note: If your springform pan has lost some of its spring, cover the bottom and halfway up the sides with foil to prevent any leaking batter from landing on the bottom of your oven and burning.

incredible cuisine

Low-Fat Daiquiri Cheesecake

RUM and lime combine here in a slightly frozen creation—now you know where I got this name!

makes 16 slices

8 to 10 ounces lemon cookies
1 tablespoon pure vanilla extract
1 tablespoon rum
nonstick cooking spray

the cake filling

24 ounces low-fat cream cheese, softened
8 ounces low-fat sour cream
4 eggs
1 cup sugar, divided
$^1/_4$ cup freshly squeezed lime juice (2 limes)
1 tablespoon pure vanilla extract
$^1/_2$ teaspoon pure lemon extract
4 egg whites

To make the crust, crumble the cookies and mix in the vanilla and rum. Spray a 9-inch springform pan with the non-stick cooking spray and press the cookie mixture evenly and firmly onto the bottom of the pan.

Preheat oven to 325°F.

Use an electric mixer to beat the cream cheese until smooth. On low speed, add the sour cream. Add the eggs, $^1/_2$ cup of the sugar, the lime juice, and the vanilla and lemon extracts.

In a separate bowl, use an electric mixer with clean, dry beaters to beat the egg whites. Start at low speed and increase the speed as peaks form. Slowly add the remaining $^1/_2$ cup of sugar. When the beaten whites have soft peaks (stiff but not dry), fold them gently into the filling. Do not overmix!

Pour the mixture into prepared pan and bake for approximately 1 hour, until the cake has risen and browned slightly and it just shimmies when you gently move the pan. It's a good idea to place the springform on a low, flat pan or foil to catch any batter that leaks. Turn the heat off and let the cake stand in the oven for 1 more hour. Remove the cake from the oven and cool it before serving for at least 12 hours in the refrigerator or, better yet, leave it in the freezer overnight.

Chocolate & Almond-Coated Pears

NOW this is not a particularly easy dessert to make. But it will be very impressive and beautiful on your table. One important thing to remember: The pears must be very, very dry, or else whatever you try to put on them will slide right off. Also, do not worry if the pears are not ripe. They will ripen as they cook in the wine.

makes 4 servings

1 bottle White Zinfandel or other light, fruity blush wine

¼ cup lemon juice

6 whole cloves

1 cinnamon stick

4 large pears

1 cup heavy cream

12 ounces semisweet chocolate, broken into small pieces

8 ounces roasted almonds, chopped

Vanilla Crème Anglaise (recipe on page 255)

In a large saucepan, bring the wine, lemon juice, cloves, and cinnamon to a boil.

In the meantime, peel and core the pears, leaving the stems intact. Immediately immerse the pears in the heated wine, cover and cook for approximately 25 minutes, or until the pears are tender.

Remove the pears from the wine and drain them on paper towels. Dry them as much as possible and set them aside on a wire rack set over a pan.

In a saucepan, heat the cream. Add the chocolate pieces and whisk until the mixture is smooth.

Carefully pour enough chocolate over the pears to coat the entire fruit. As soon as they are covered, sprinkle them with the toasted almonds and carefully transfer them to a serving plate.

Serve cold with the Vanilla Crème Anglaise.

Frozen Lemon & Orange Soufflé

THIS is one of the silkiest ice creams I've ever had in my life. And the sauce—mama mia, you will lick the bowl clean!

makes 4 servings

4 oranges
6 eggs, separated
1 cup sugar, divided
6 ounces lemon curd or lemon marmalade
$1/2$ cup Curaçao, Grand Marnier, or other orange liqueur
1 tablespoon pure vanilla extract
2 cups heavy cream
Lime & Yogurt Sauce (recipe below)

Using a "channel" knife, cut a few grooves into the orange peels. Cut the tops off the oranges and reserve. Empty the entire fruit of the orange pulp, being careful not to create a hole in the bottom. Freeze the empty orange "shells."

In a bowl, combine the egg yolks with $1/2$ cup of the sugar and beat until thick and a pale yellow. If using an electric mixer, mix for 5 to 7 minutes. Add the lemon curd or marmalade, orange liqueur, and vanilla. Mix well.

In a separate cold bowl, whip the cream until firm. Set aside.

In another bowl at room temperature, beat the egg whites until soft peaks form.

In a large stainless steel bowl, blend the whipped cream and the egg yolk mixture.

GENTLY fold in the egg whites. Transfer the mixture to a pastry bag fitted with a large tip.

Pipe the mixture into the orange shells, extending 1 inch higher than the top of the orange. Freeze for at least 4 to 5 hours. Add the tops and serve right out of the freezer with the Lime & Yogurt Sauce.

lime & yogurt sauce

12 ounces low-fat vanilla yogurt
6 ounces lime or lemon curd
1 tablespoon pure vanilla extract

Mix all the ingredients in a food processor until very smooth.

Cinnamon Apple Strudel

OOOH—this is an irresistible dessert! It is very simple to make, and the presentation is stunning. Feel free to use different fruits, if you like; pears or peaches would also be great in this recipe.

makes 4 servings

5 tablespoons butter, divided

4 Granny Smith apples, peeled, cored, and cut into $1/2$-inch cubes

$1/4$ cup dark brown sugar

3 tablespoons fresh lemon juice

$1/2$ teaspoon ground cinnamon

$1/2$ teaspoon ground allspice

$1/2$ cup raisins, soaked in $1/2$ cup dark rum and drained

6 phyllo pastry sheets

2 tablespoons confectioners' sugar

Vanilla Crème Anglaise (recipe on page 255)

In a large sauté pan, heat 2 tablespoons of the butter until foamy. Add the apples and cook until soft, 5 to 7 minutes. Add the brown sugar, lemon juice, cinnamon, allspice, and the drained raisins. Cook until the apples are cooked throughout. Set in a glass bowl and cool for at least 1 hour.

Preheat oven to 375°F.

Melt the remaining 3 tablespoons butter in a small saucepan.

Pull out 3 sheets of pastry at a time, keeping the rest of the dough covered with a slightly dampened towel (to keep it from drying out). Place the 3 sheets in front of you and, using a pastry brush, lightly brush melted butter all over the first sheet. Starting 2 inches from the edge of the short side of the first sheet, spoon out approximately $1/2$ cup of the apple mixture in a line. Begin rolling the dough slowly, away from you, making a tight roll. Butter sheet #2 at the end and place the stuffed roll on the edge of this sheet and roll both toward you. Continue the same procedure with sheet #3, rolling away from you again. You have one roll of 3 pastry sheets.

Butter, stuff, and roll the second strudel. Set both strudels on a nonstick baking sheet. Brush the tops lightly with melted butter. Bake for 7 to 10 minutes until the phyllo is a nice golden brown.

Let cool for 5 minutes. Sift the confectioners' sugar on the tops. Slice with a serrated knife and serve while hot with the Vanilla Crème Anglaise .

Almond Baskets Filled with Mixed Berries, Vanilla Crème Anglaise & Raspberry Coulis

THESE really look like little baskets! It's an absolutely gorgeous and—believe it or not—a rather simple dessert. Read all the directions first, and then proceed very carefully, making one basket at a time. Make them ahead only if you have a VERY dry area in which to store them.

makes 4 to 6 baskets

15 ounces toasted almonds, crumbled

1 cup sugar

$^1\!/_2$ cup (1 stick) butter

3 tablespoons flour

2 tablespoons corn syrup

2 tablespoons heavy cream

2 pints mixed berries

fresh mint leaves for garnish

mixed fresh berries

Vanilla Crème Anglaise (recipe on page 255)

Raspberry Coulis (recipe on page 254)

Preheat oven to 375°F.

In a glass bowl, mix the almonds, sugar, butter, flour, corn syrup, and cream. Chill in the refrigerator for 1 hour.

On a nonstick baking sheet, using an ice-cream scoop, place about 2 rounded tablespoons of the batter in the center of the sheet. Spread it with the back of a spoon until it is approximately 3 inches round. Place the baking sheet on the center rack of the oven and bake until golden brown throughout (approximately 10 minutes). Bake only one basket at a time.

Wait 30 seconds but no longer. Using a large metal spatula, scoop the "basket" off the baking sheet in a curling motion and place it immediately inside a coffee cup. Let it cool in the cup until it holds its shape. (If you wait too long to place the cookie in the cup, return it to the hot oven for a few seconds to soften it again.) Continue until all the baskets are made.

Fill the baskets with your favorite berries and garnish with mint. Serve with both the Vanilla Crème Anglaise and the Raspberry Coulis.

incredible cuisine

stocks & sauces

By now you're probably tired of hearing me say it: If you want to prepare delicious food, "incredible" food, you absolutely must start with the right ingredients. And, without a doubt, that includes homemade stock. Until you try it yourself, you just won't believe the difference it makes in your soups and sauces; at least 50 percent of the flavor—maybe even 75 percent!—comes from the stock.

You'll see that many of my recipes call for stock, and I have found that the only way for me to keep enough on hand is to set aside a day, every month or so, to stay home and fill up my freezer. Believe it or not, these days turn out to be so relaxing! I putter around the house getting things done, while the vegetables and the chicken, beef, or duck bones simmer away on the stove. I'll often make my pestos then, too, and maybe a coulis, and then I freeze all of it in containers ranging from ice cube trays to plastic tubs.

If you're looking for the one thing you can do to get better results in the kitchen, this is it. Commit to a "stock day" of your own. The investment of just a little time will pay off every time you cook!

Beef Stock

BEEF bones are not a standard supermarket item, so ask the butcher to save some for you.

makes about 2 quarts

4 pounds beef bones

2 medium onions, skin left on, cut into chunks

1 pound veal trimmings (optional; not needed if bones are very meaty)

1 leek, rinsed well to remove grit, cut into 1-inch pieces (use white and green parts)

2 carrots, cut into 1-inch pieces

2 celery stalks, cut into 1-inch pieces (remove leaves)

2 tomatoes, cut into 8 wedges

3 sprigs fresh parsley, including stems

3 sprigs fresh thyme

1 large bay leaf

6 black peppercorns

Preheat oven to 400°F.

Place the bones (in a single layer) and the onions in a large roasting pan. If you are using veal trimmings, scatter them around the bones. Roast in the oven for 1 hour until bones are golden brown on all sides. Remove pan from the oven and transfer browned bones to a large stockpot.

Add all remaining ingredients and enough cold water to cover by 2 inches. Bring to a boil, then reduce the heat so that the mixture just bubbles at a gentle simmer, and cook for 8 to 12 hours. Turn off the heat and let the stock cool down for 1 hour so that it's easier to handle.

Don't worry about removing the fat floating on top of the stock. It will help keep the stock fresh by forming a seal in the refrigerator or freezer, and it will be easier to remove before you reheat the stock.

When the stock has cooled a bit, use a slotted spoon or tongs to remove the bones and discard. Strain the stock through a fine sieve, then strain again through a sieve or a colander lined with a double layer of cheesecloth to remove any small particles.

Portion the stock into containers—from ice cube trays to pints or quarts—and let it cool. Label and date containers, then freeze.

Note: Once you've made a nice brown beef stock, you can easily turn it into a *demi-glace*. Simply cook the strained stock in a large saucepan until its volume has reduced by half and it forms a syrupy liquid. This takes up less room in the refrigerator or freezer, and it's easy to scoop out a tablespoon or two as you need it for a sauce. If you'd like to go the final step and produce a true *glace de viande*, or meat glaze, transfer the *demi-glace* to a smaller saucepan and cook again gently until the volume has reduced by half. When cooled, this will form a gelatinous mixture that has an extremely concentrated flavor.

Roasted Chicken Stock

THE bones and vegetables are roasted to a beautiful dark golden color, creating a light golden brown stock with an outstanding nutlike flavor.

makes about 2 quarts

4 to 5 pounds chicken bones and parts (backs, necks, carcasses, thighs)

2 medium onions, unpeeled and coarsely chopped

1/2 cup tomato paste

4 celery stalks, cut into 1/2-inch chunks (remove leaves)

3 carrots, scrubbed and cut into 1/2-inch chunks

1 leek, rinsed well to remove grit, cut into 1/2-inch pieces (use green and white parts)

12 sprigs fresh parsley, including stems

4 sprigs fresh thyme

2 large bay leaves

12 black peppercorns

Preheat oven to 450°F.

In a roasting pan, combine the chicken parts, onions, and tomato paste. Roast for about 45 minutes, or until golden brown. Transfer to a large stockpot. Add the celery, carrots, leeks, parsley, thyme, bay leaves, and peppercorns. Add enough cold water to cover all the ingredients (approximately 3 to 4 quarts). Bring the water to a boil very slowly. This will help prevent clouding of the stock. Do not cover the pot. When the stock comes to a boil, lower the heat so that the stock simmers—just bubbles gently. Skim the froth and foam from the surface, using a slotted spoon.

Let the stock simmer for about 4 hours, skimming as needed. You don't have to stand around in the kitchen and supervise the stock as it cooks.

Turn off the heat and let the stock cool for 30 minutes to 1 hour. Use a slotted spoon to remove the chicken bones and discard. Then, strain the stock through a fine sieve and discard the vegetables left behind. Strain again, this time through a sieve or colander lined with a double layer of cheesecloth.

Cool overnight in the refrigerator, to allow the fat to rise to the surface. Skim the fat and portion the stock into containers—from ice cube trays to pints or quarts. Label and date containers, then freeze.

Chicken Stock

I have been making this chicken stock for 30 years. It is a simple but important ingredient in low-fat cooking.

makes about 2 quarts

4 pounds chicken bones and parts (backs, necks, carcasses, thighs)

3 quarts cold water

2 medium onions, peeled and coarsely chopped

2 carrots, scrubbed and cut into $1/2$-inch chunks

2 celery stalks, cut into $1/2$-inch chunks (remove leaves)

2 tomatoes, cut into chunks

1 leek, rinsed well to remove grit, cut into $1/2$-inch pieces (use green and white parts)

3 sprigs fresh parsley, including stems

3 sprigs fresh thyme

1 large bay leaf

6 black peppercorns

Rinse the chicken parts in cold water, then put them in a large stockpot. Add cold water, then place the pot over medium-low heat and slowly bring to a boil. This will help prevent clouding of the stock. Don't cover the pot. When the stock is boiling, reduce the heat so that the stock simmers—just bubbles gently—and skim the froth and foam from the surface, using a slotted spoon.

Let the stock simmer for about 4 hours, skimming as needed. You don't have to stand around in the kitchen and supervise the stock as it cooks.

After 4 hours, add the vegetables, herbs, and spices and cook 1 more hour. Turn off the heat and let the stock cool for 30 minutes to 1 hour. Use a slotted spoon to remove the chicken bones—they will be falling apart by now—and discard. Then, strain the stock through a fine sieve and discard the vegetables left behind. Strain again, this time through a sieve or colander lined with a double layer of cheesecloth.

Cool the stock overnight in the refrigerator, to allow all the fat to rise to the surface. Skim the fat and portion the stock into containers—from ice cube trays to pints or quarts, label and date containers, then freeze.

Duck Stock

IN addition to succulent meat and a crispy skin, roast duck yields another great by-product: a carcass just waiting to be simmered into this savory stock.

makes 3 cups

- 1 carcass from a roasted 4¼- to 5-pound duck, plus uncooked neck, wing tips, and giblets
- 2 medium onions, quartered
- 2 medium carrots, cut into 1-inch pieces
- 1 leek, washed and cut into 1-inch pieces
- 3 celery stalks, cut into 1-inch pieces
- 2 sprigs fresh thyme
- 2 sprigs fresh rosemary
- 2 bay leaves
- 12 black peppercorns

Preheat oven to 400°F.

Discard any excess fat from the roasted duck carcass. With a large knife or cleaver, chop the carcass into 4 or 5 pieces and place in a roasting pan with the reserved neck, wing tips, and giblets. Add the onions and carrots.

Roast for 30 to 45 minutes, until lightly browned. Again, pour off any fat and transfer all the ingredients to a stockpot. Add enough water to cover, about 10 cups. Add 1 cup of water to the roasting pan and set over medium-high heat on the stovetop. Bring to a boil, scraping the pan bottom of any browned bits, and add these juices and bits to the stockpot. Add the celery, leeks, thyme, rosemary, bay leaves, and peppercorns. Bring to a boil.

Skim any foam from the surface, reduce the heat to low, and let simmer, uncovered, for about 2 hours. Be sure to skim the surface every 30 minutes. Strain the stock through a very fine sieve and return to a clean saucepan. Cook over medium-high heat until only 3 cups of the liquid remains. The stock can be covered and refrigerated for up to 3 days and frozen for up to 6 months.

Bouillabaisse Stock

THIS outstanding stock is the main ingredient in my Florida Bouillabaisse (recipe on page 144). But you can also use it in any fish or seafood dish that calls for chicken stock. And, it's the perfect base for a light and healthy pasta dish.

makes 2 quarts

2 cups Chardonnay or other full-bodied, dry white wine

1 tablespoon saffron threads (approximately)

1 tablespoon extra-virgin olive oil

1 onion, diced

1 leek, rinsed well to remove grit, diced (use white and green parts)

1 head of fennel, diced

6 cups fish stock or Chicken Stock (recipe on page 240)

2 cups chopped tomatoes

2 tablespoons tomato paste

6 sprigs fresh thyme

grated zest of 1 orange

2 bay leaves

Make the saffron infusion: In a saucepan, bring the wine to a boil. Add the saffron and let reduce until only $3/4$ cup of the wine remains. Set aside.

In the meantime, in a stockpot, heat the olive oil and add the onions. Sweat the onions for 2 minutes. Add the leeks and fennel and cook for 2 more minutes. Add the stock, tomatoes, tomato paste, thyme, orange zest, and bay leaves. Add the saffron infusion and cook for 30 more minutes. Transfer to a blender in batches and process until very smooth. Strain through a fine sieve.

Quick Stock:

Add the saffron infusion to a good chicken stock with 2 tablespoons tomato paste and fresh thyme. Cook for 15 minutes. Strain.

Madeira Mushroom Sauce

makes 2 cups

- 1 tablespoon extra-virgin olive oil
- 2 tablespoons minced shallots
- $^1/_4$ cup balsamic vinegar
- 2 cups mushrooms (cremini, shiitake, or oyster), sliced
- 2 tablespoons chopped fresh tarragon
- 1 tablespoon chopped fresh thyme
- 1 cup Madeira wine
- 2 cups Roasted Chicken Stock (recipe on page 239)
- salt & freshly ground black pepper to taste
- 1 tablespoon cornstarch mixed with 2 tablespoons water

In a saucepan, heat the olive oil, then add the shallots. When they become golden brown, add the vinegar. Let reduce until all the vinegar has evaporated. Stir in the mushrooms and fresh herbs. Cook for 3 minutes. Add the wine and cook until reduced by half. Pour in the stock and adjust seasoning with salt and pepper. Mix stir in the cornstarch mixture. Cook for an additional 15 minutes and serve.

Tomato, Capers & Black Olive Sauce

B E sure to use imported niçoise or Kalamata olives.

makes 2$^1/_2$ cups

- 1 tablespoon extra-virgin olive oil
- $^1/_4$ cup minced white onions
- 1 tablespoon minced fresh garlic
- 1 tablespoon fresh thyme leaves, chopped
- 1$^3/_4$ pounds ripe tomatoes, peeled, seeded, and chopped, to make 2 cups
- 1 cup Chicken Stock (recipe on page 240)
- $^1/_4$ cup black niçoise olives, chopped
- $^1/_4$ cup nonpareil capers
- salt & freshly ground black pepper to taste

In a saucepan, heat the olive oil and when hot, add the onions. Cook until translucent, then add the garlic. When the garlic becomes fragrant, add the tomatoes, stock, and thyme. Cook for 10 minutes and stir in the black olives and capers. Season with salt and pepper.

Barbecue Sauce

I have tried just about every barbecue sauce available, and none of them has really satisfied my taste buds, except this one. Try it—I bet you'll love it!

makes about 2¹/₂ cups

1 tablespoon extra-virgin olive oil

¹/₂ cup finely chopped yellow onions

¹/₂ cup chopped leeks

2 jalapeño peppers, seeded and diced

1 green bell pepper, diced very fine

1 red bell pepper, diced very fine

1 garlic clove, chopped

2 cups ketchup

2 cups chopped tomatoes

1 cup Roasted Chicken Stock (recipe on page 239)

¹/₂ cup dark brown sugar

¹/₄ cup white wine vinegar

3 to 4 tablespoons chili sauce

3 tablespoons Worcestershire sauce

1 teaspoon dried mustard

³/₄ teaspoon Liquid Smoke

In a large, heavy-duty saucepan, heat the olive oil. Add the onions and sweat them for 5 minutes until a golden brown. Add the leeks and all the peppers and sweat them for 2 minutes. Add the garlic and when it becomes fragrant, sauté for 2 more minutes. Add all the remaining ingredients. Let reduce on medium to low heat for 20 minutes.

Transfer the sauce to a blender and purée until smooth. For extra-smooth texture, strain through a fine sieve.

Kalamata Olive Sauce

1 tablespoon extra-virgin olive oil

1 shallot, minced

¹/₂ cup port wine

1 cup Roasted Chicken Stock (recipe on page 239)

1 pound tomatoes, peeled, seeded, and chopped into ¹/₄-inch cubes, to make 1 cup

¹/₂ cup imported black olives, such as Kalamata, pitted and chopped

2 tablespoons snipped fresh chives

1 tablespoon cornstarch mixed with 1 tablespoon water

In a small saucepan, heat the olive oil, add the shallots, and sauté until golden brown. Pour in the port wine and the stock. Reduce for 2 minutes. Add the tomatoes, olives, chives, and the cornstarch mixture. Cook for 2 minutes until the sauce is thick enough to coat the back of a spoon.

Wild Mushroom & Cabernet Sauce

FEEL free to substitute any mushroom for the shiitake, oyster, or cremini.

makes 1¹/₂ cups

1 tablespoon extra-virgin olive oil

6 ounces wild mushrooms (shiitake, oyster, or cremini)

2 tablespoons chopped shallots

1 teaspoon chopped fresh sage

1 cup Cabernet Sauvignon or other full-bodied red wine

2 cups Beef Stock or Roasted Chicken Stock (recipes on pages 238 and 239)

1 teaspoon cornstarch mixed with 1 tablespoon water

In a sauté pan, heat the olive oil. Add the mushrooms, shallots, and sage and sweat them for 2 minutes. Pour in the wine. Cook until reduced by two-thirds. Add the stock and reduce by half.

Check the sauce for consistency and flavor; it may need to reduce further. Add the cornstarch mixture to thicken, as necessary. Do not strain.

Spiced Tomato & Basil Sauce

makes 2¹/₂ cups

1 tablespoon extra-virgin olive oil

¹/₂ cup finely diced onions

¹/₄ cup finely diced celery

¹/₄ cup finely diced leeks

¹/₄ Scotch bonnet chile pepper*

1 teaspoon minced fresh garlic

1³/₄ pounds ripe tomatoes, peeled, seeded, and chopped, to make 2 cups

¹/₄ cup fresh basil leaves, sliced chiffonade (thin ribbons)

1 cup Chicken Stock (recipe on page 240)

salt & freshly ground black pepper to taste

In a medium saucepan, heat the olive oil. Add the onions and when translucent, add the celery and leeks. Cook for 5 minutes. Add the Scotch bonnet chile and garlic. When the garlic becomes fragrant (30 to 45 seconds), add the tomatoes and basil. Cook for 2 minutes. Pour in the stock and cook for just a few minutes. Season with salt and pepper and serve immediately.

*If Scotch bonnet peppers are not available, substitute with a couple of dashes of Tabasco sauce.

Currant & Pinot Noir Sauce

makes 2½ cups

1 tablespoon extra-virgin olive oil

4 ounces pancetta (Italian cured bacon), diced

4 ounces 97% fat-free smoked ham, diced

1 cup diced onions

2 tablespoons fresh thyme leaves, chopped

2 tablespoons minced garlic

2 cups Pinot Noir

2 cups Beef Stock (recipe on page 238)

4 ounces black or red currant jelly

2 tablespoons cornstarch mixed with 2 tablespoons water

In a saucepan, heat the olive oil, then add the pancetta and ham. Sauté for approximately 5 minutes. Add the onions and cook until golden brown. Add the thyme and garlic. Sauté for 30 seconds. Pour in the wine and cook until reduced by half. Add the currant jelly, stock, and the cornstarch mixture. Cook slowly for approximately 35 to 45 minutes.

Thai Curry Sauce

makes 1½ cups

1 can Thai coconut milk

1 teaspoon Thai curry paste

½ teaspoon turmeric

1 tablespoon chopped fresh cilantro

salt & freshly ground black pepper to taste

In a saucepan over medium heat, reduce the coconut milk until it is thick enough to coat the back of a spoon. Add the rest of the ingredients. Whisk all together and pour into a serving bowl.

Roasted Garlic & Tomato Sauce

USE the largest and freshest garlic bulb you can find.

makes 2¹/₂ cups

1 whole garlic head

2 tablespoons extra-virgin olive oil & 2 teaspoons for drizzling on the garlic

1 cup diced onions

1 cup diced celery

1³/₄ pounds ripe tomatoes, peeled, seeded, and chopped, to make 2 cups OR one 28-ounce can recipe-ready tomatoes, drained

¹/₄ cup tomato purée

1 cup Chicken Stock (recipe on page 240)

2 tablespoons chopped fresh basil leaves

1 tablespoon chopped fresh oregano leaves

2 tablespoons chopped fresh cilantro leaves

salt & freshly ground black pepper to taste

To Roast the Garlic:

Heat oven to 375°F.

Do not remove the papery outer skin from the garlic. With a very sharp knife, cut the garlic head in half lengthwise. Set the garlic halves, cut side up, on a piece of foil, then drizzle each half with 1 teaspoon of olive oil. Close the foil and roast for about 45 minutes, or until tender and buttery. When cool, slip the cloves from the skin.

In a saucepan, heat 1 tablespoon of olive oil and when hot, add the onions. When the onions are translucent, add the celery and sweat them for 2 minutes. Add the tomatoes, tomato purée, stock, basil, oregano, and roasted garlic. Let simmer on low heat for 15 minutes.

Using an immersion blender, blend until very smooth. Strain through a medium sieve. Add the cilantro. Adjust the seasoning with salt and pepper.

Herb Cream Cheese

makes 8 ounces

8 ounces low-fat cream cheese, softened

1 tablespoon minced fresh garlic

1 teaspoon chopped fresh thyme leaves

1 teaspoon chopped fresh oregano leaves

¹/₄ teaspoon salt

¹/₄ teaspoon freshly ground black pepper

In a bowl, blend the cream cheese with the garlic, thyme, oregano, salt, and pepper. Refrigerate.

Champagne Mustard Sauce

IF you can't find Meaux mustard, use regular Dijon mustard. But add about 1 teaspoon of whole mustard seeds along with the ginger.

makes 1 cup

1 tablespoon extra-virgin olive oil

2 shallots, minced

1 tablespoon fresh chopped ginger

$^1/_2$ cup Champagne

2 tablespoons low-sodium soy sauce

$^1/_2$ cup bottled clam juice

$^1/_2$ cup evaporated skim milk

1 teaspoon cornstarch mixed with 1 tablespoon water

2 tablespoons snipped chives

2 tablespoons grainy mustard, preferably moutarde de Meaux

salt & freshly ground black pepper to taste

In a saucepan, heat the olive oil and when hot, add the shallots. When they are golden brown, add the ginger and cook for 1 minute. Add the Champagne and soy sauce and let reduce by half. Pour in the clam juice and bring to a boil. Lower the heat and add the evaporated milk and cornstarch mixture. Stir in the chives, mustard, salt and pepper. Cook for 2 to 3 minutes and serve.

Mustard & Balsamic Vinaigrette

THIS is not an emulsified vinaigrette, so do not use a blender.

makes 1 cup

$^1/_4$ cup extra-virgin olive oil

1 tablespoon Dijon mustard

1 tablespoon balsamic vinegar

1 tablespoon honey

3 tablespoons hot water

1 tablespoon chopped fresh basil

$^1/_4$ teaspoon salt

$^1/_2$ teaspoon freshly ground black pepper

In a glass bowl, mix all the ingredients with a fork.

Sun-Dried Tomato Pesto

FEEL free to double up on the basil if you can't get cilantro.

makes about 2 cups

1 cup fresh basil leaves, tightly packed

$^1/_2$ cup fresh cilantro leaves, tightly packed

$^1/_2$ cup freshly grated Reggiano Parmesan cheese

$^1/_2$ cup extra-virgin olive oil

$^1/_4$ cup sun-dried tomatoes, reconstituted

$^1/_4$ cup toasted pine nuts

$^1/_4$ cup Chicken Stock (recipe on page 240)

4 garlic cloves, chopped

1 tablespoon apple-cider vinegar

$^1/_4$ teaspoon salt

$^1/_4$ teaspoon freshly ground black pepper

Blend all the ingredients in a food processor to a smooth paste.

Almond Pesto

THIS pesto has only a fraction of the fat of the traditional recipe—but ALL the flavor and texture!

makes about 2 cups

2 cups fresh basil leaves, tightly packed

$^3/_4$ cup extra-virgin olive oil

$^1/_2$ cup toasted almonds

$^1/_2$ cup freshly grated Reggiano Parmesan cheese

$^1/_4$ cup Chicken Stock (recipe on page 240)

6 garlic cloves, chopped

1 tablespoon balsamic vinegar

$^1/_4$ teaspoon freshly ground black pepper

In a food processor, combine all the ingredients and blend until the pesto looks like a coarse paste.

Broccoli Pesto

YOU can always make pesto ahead and freeze it in ice cube trays. It melts very quickly!

makes about 2 cups

1 cup tightly packed fresh basil leaves

³/₄ cup extra-virgin olive oil

¹/₂ cup freshly grated Reggiano Parmesan cheese

¹/₂ cup tightly packed broccoli florets

¹/₂ cup blanched almonds

¹/₄ cup Chicken Stock (recipe on page 240)

6 garlic cloves, chopped

1 tablespoon balsamic vinegar

¹/₄ teaspoon freshly ground black pepper

Combine all the ingredients in a food processor and blend until you have a smooth paste.

Chile Pepper Glaze

makes 1¹/₂ cups

1 tablespoon sesame oil

2 tablespoons minced shallots

¹/₄ small Scotch bonnet pepper, diced very fine

¹/₄ small jalapeño pepper, diced very fine

¹/₄ cup rice-wine vinegar

¹/₂ cup port wine

1 cup Chicken or Duck Stock (recipes on pages 240 and 241)

2 tablespoons corn syrup

1 tablespoon honey

1 teaspoon cornstarch mixed with 1 tablespoon water

salt & freshly ground black pepper to taste

In a saucepan, heat the sesame oil. When hot, add the shallots and peppers. When the shallots are translucent, add the rice-wine vinegar. Let reduce until almost dry. Add the port wine and let reduce by half. Add the stock, the corn syrup, and honey.

Adjust the seasoning with salt and pepper.

Smoked Ham Relish

$1/4$ cup diced **97%** fat-free smoked ham

I garlic clove, minced

I large shallot, minced

$1/4$ cup pitted niçoise olives, chopped

$1/4$ cup chopped tomatoes

I tablespoon extra-virgin olive oil

I tablespoon rice-wine vinegar

$1/2$ cup Chicken Stock (recipe on page 240)

I teaspoon minced fresh basil

I teaspoon minced fresh parsley

salt & freshly ground black pepper to taste

In a nonstick pan over very low heat, cook the diced ham until light brown in color. Add the garlic and shallots and sauté for I minute. Transfer the sautéed mixture to a bowl. Add all the remaining ingredients and mix well.

Tomato & Cucumber Relish

THIS is a perfect companion for stuffed shrimp or any grilled chicken or fish dish. Be sure to cut the tomatoes and cucumbers into small cubes no larger than $1/4$ inch.

$1 1/2$ pounds ripe tomatoes, peeled, seeded, and cut into small cubes, to make 2 cups

I cup diced European cucumbers

I tablespoon balsamic vinegar

$1/2$ cup cubed red onions

2 tablespoons small capers

2 tablespoons extra-virgin olive oil

$1/4$ cup chopped fresh mint leaves

salt & freshly ground black pepper to taste

Mix all the ingredients in a bowl, just minutes before serving.

Papaya, Mango & Pineapple Relish

makes 2 cups

$^1/_2$ cup diced papaya

$^1/_2$ cup diced mango

$^1/_2$ cup diced pineapple

2 tablespoons finely chopped fresh cilantro

1 tablespoon finely chopped fresh mint leaves

1 tablespoon apple-cider vinegar

1 tablespoon extra-virgin olive oil

$^1/_4$ teaspoon salt

$^1/_4$ teaspoon freshly ground black pepper

Gently toss all the ingredients together to preserve their texture.

Giblet & Apple Brandy Gravy

makes 3 cups

1 tablespoon extra-virgin olive oil

turkey neck and giblets

1 cup chopped onions

2 chopped shallots

$^1/_4$ cup apple brandy

$^1/_4$ cup flour

3 cups Chicken Stock (recipe on page 240)

1 teaspoon fresh sage, chopped

1 teaspoon fresh thyme, chopped

salt & freshly ground black pepper to taste

In a large saucepan, heat the olive oil. When hot, add the turkey neck and giblets. Sauté for 5 minutes. Add the onions and when golden brown, add the shallots. Sweat the shallots for 2 more minutes.

Add the brandy and ignite it. Let all the alcohol burn off. Add the flour and stock. Cook for 30 minutes. Remove from the heat and strain through a fine sieve. Return to the heat and add the fresh herbs. Cook for an additional 15 minutes.

Adjust the seasoning with salt and pepper.

Roasted Bell Pepper Coulis

makes 1 3/4 cups

2 red or green bell peppers

1 cup Chicken Stock (recipe on page 240)

1 tablespoon chopped fresh garlic

12 basil leaves

salt & freshly ground black pepper to taste

Roast the bell peppers: Place the peppers on an open gas burner until the skin blisters and turns completely black. You can achieve the same result on a grill or under the broiler in the oven. Transfer the peppers to a plastic bag and close securely to let them steam for 20 minutes. Scrape off the charred skin, then remove the stems and seeds. Try to remove all without rinsing the pepper under water, as you would lose too much of the roasted flavor.

In a food processor, combine the peppers, stock, garlic, and basil. Process until very smooth. Adjust the seasoning with salt and pepper.

Mango Coulis

makes 2 cups

1 pound fresh mangoes, peeled and chopped

3/4 cup freshly squeezed orange juice

1/4 cup orange juice concentrate

1/2 cup sugar

1/4 cup tequila

2 tablespoons freshly squeezed lemon juice

In a food processor, combine all the ingredients. Blend until very smooth. Strain through a fine sieve for a smooth, even consistency.

Raspberry Coulis

makes 2¹/₂ cups

2 cups fresh raspberries OR two 10-ounce packages frozen, thawed and drained

¹/₄ cup sugar

¹/₄ cup freshly squeezed orange juice

2 tablespoons freshly squeezed lemon juice

2 tablespoons Chambord liqueur

Place the berries, sugar, and orange and lemon juices in a blender and purée until very smooth.

Strain through a fine sieve into a glass bowl, pressing on the solids to extract all the juices.

Stir in the Chambord, taste and adjust the sugar to your liking.

Apricot & Orange Coulis

makes 3 cups

1 pound fresh apricots OR 8 ounces dried apricots, marinated in ¹/₄ cup Curaçao or other orange liqueur

³/₄ cup freshly squeezed orange juice

¹/₄ cup orange juice concentrate

¹/₂ cup sugar

2 tablespoons freshly squeezed lemon juice

¹/₂ cup orange segments

If using dried apricots, marinate them overnight in the Curaçao.

In a food processor, combine the apricots, orange juice, orange juice concentrate, sugar, and lemon juice. Blend until very smooth. Strain through a fine sieve for a smooth consistency. Add the orange segments.

Port Wine & Raspberry Sauce

IF you aren't watching your fat intake, go ahead and use regular yogurt in this easy-to-prepare sauce—a perfect companion to any chocolate dessert.

makes 2¹/₂ cups

1 cup fresh raspberries
1¹/₂ cups nonfat yogurt
¹/₄ cup port wine
2 tablespoons sugar (optional)

In a food processor, blend all the ingredients until very smooth. Strain, if necessary.

Vanilla Crème Anglaise

makes 2 cups

1¹/₂ cups heavy cream
1 vanilla bean, split lengthwise
3 tablespoons sugar
3 egg yolks

In a nonreactive saucepan, scald the cream and vanilla bean. Remove from the heat, cover, and let the flavors infuse for 20 minutes. Remove the bean, rinse it and save for another use.

In a medium bowl, beat the sugar and egg yolks until pale yellow in color. Add 2 to 3 ounces of the cream mixture to the egg mixture and mix well.

Slowly pour in the rest of the cream. Transfer the mixture back to the saucepan and heat over medium heat for about 10 minutes. Stir constantly with a wooden spoon until mixture becomes thick enough to coat the back of a spoon. (When you run your finger across the back of a spoon, the mark of your finger should remain.)

Immediately strain through a fine strainer into a glass bowl and whisk for 1 minute to release the heat.

Cool for at least 3 to 4 hours in the refrigerator.

entertaining

I have one important rule to give you about entertaining: Relax! It is so easy to let the food take control of you; I do it myself, sometimes. But you must remember why you're entertaining, why you invited your family or friends to come over for a meal. You wanted to see them, to be with them, to share delicious food, yes, but mostly to share each other's company. As one of my friends used to say, "Your guests did not come to see a chicken. They came to see you."

One thing that may help you stay calm when you entertain is to write out a "count-down." This is something we do at my restaurant when we have a big party or a special dinner coming up. We start with the time the event will begin and work backward, making a list of all the things we have to do and when. This will help give you the sense that you have everything under control. Otherwise you'll waste a lot of time and energy wondering what you forgot!

Romantic Dinner for Two

It would not be very romantic to leave your special guest alone in the dining room, waiting for you while you "work up a sweat" in the kitchen, would it? This menu is perfect for that type of evening. The cannelloni, which can be prepared in advance, can go directly from your refrigerator into the oven and will be done in only 10 minutes. Have the Roasted Bell Pepper Coulis waiting in a small saucepan on the stove; you can warm that over medium heat while the cannelloni is in the oven. You could also put the potato crust on the salmon ahead of time, and have it ready in a buttered ovenproof pan. Pop it into the oven as you are finishing the appetizer. At the same time, you can warm the Chives and Scallion Sauce on medium heat on the stove (but don't add the milk and cornstarch until right before serving the fish). It will take only 2 minutes to finish the sauce.

Prepare the Baked Carrots in advance and reheat them in the oven along with the fish.

The crème brûlée can be waiting in the refrigerator. Just sprinkle the sugar on top at the last minute.

TURKEY CANNELLONI WRAPPED IN PHYLLO PASTRY
with Roasted Bell Pepper Coulis (*page 34*)
෴
POTATO-CRUSTED SALMON
with Chives & Scallion Sauce (*page 150*)
෴
BAKED CARROTS (*page 193*)
෴
VANILLA & RASPBERRY CRÉME BRÛLÉE (*page 214*)
෴

Dinner for One

You may not often feel like cooking for yourself, but trust me—there is nothing quite as therapeutic as an afternoon around great food. You should prepare the custard first and refrigerate it. Next, make the pesto for the pizza, and then chop all the ingredients for the pizza and the chicken. After you've put the pizza together, baked it, and polished it off, you can cook the chicken.

PHYLLO PASTRY PIZZA
with Broccoli Pesto, Tomatoes & Goat Cheese (*page 58*)
➣

STIR-FRIED CHICKEN
with Wild Mushrooms & Asparagus (*page 122*)
➣

CARAMEL CUSTARD
with a Strawberry & Raspberry Sauce (*page 217*)
➣

The Ultimate Barbecue

How about injecting a bit of glamour in your next barbecue with these very elegant dishes? Most of the items can be prepared ahead of time. When your guests arrive, you just have to heat the grill and start cooking the scallops and the shrimp. The tabouli should be kept cold until just before serving.

SPICY SEA SCALLOPS ON SKEWERS (*page 22*)
➣

BARBECUE SHRIMP ON SKEWERS (*page 23*)
➣

TABOULI PROVENÇALE (*page 94*)
➣

KEY LIME SHRIMP BROCHETTE
with Mango & Rum Salsa (*page 155*)
➣

KAHLÚA & CHOCOLATE FLAN (*page 221*)
➣

New Year's Eve Celebration

This is another menu that allows you to enjoy the company of your guests, rather than being a prisoner in your kitchen. The crab cakes could be totally prepared, already seared in a pan, placed on a nonstick baking sheet, and ready to go into the oven. The relish can be made 2 to 3 hours before the party.

    The tenderloin could also be seared and sitting in an ovenproof pan, ready to be popped into the oven, and the sauce could be on the stovetop, waiting to be heated. The potatoes could be cooked almost all the way through, and reheated at the last moment.

    You could also make the almond baskets and the Vanilla Crème Anglaise in the afternoon. (But don't fill them with the berries until just before serving.)

CRAB, SALMON & SCALLOP CAKES
with Papaya, Mango & Pineapple Relish (*page 46*)

SAGE & SHIITAKE BEEF
TENDERLOIN (*page 168*)

ROASTED NOUVELLE POTATOES
WITH ROSEMARY (*page 199*)

ALMOND BASKETS FILLED
WITH MIXED BERRIES, VANILLA
CRÈME ANGLAISE & RASPBERRY
COULIS (*page 234*)

Thanksgiving Feast

This has to be the finest Thanksgiving menu we have ever served at The Left Bank. The wonderful thing is that you can so easily duplicate it at home. Make the soup two days in advance and the cheesecake the day before. If you also prepare the stuffing a day ahead, all you have to do on the big day is make the turkey and the gravy!

BUTTERNUT SQUASH & BOURBON BISQUE (*page 70*)

ROASTED TURKEY
with Cornbread & Sausage Stuffing (*page 110*)
Giblet & Apple Brandy Gravy (*page 252*)

SWEET POTATOES, PEARL ONIONS & RAISINS
with Honey & Balsamic Vinegar Glaze (*page 202*)

LOW-FAT PUMPKIN CHEESECAKE (*page 224*)

Dinner with Your Best Friends

When I have my best friends over for dinner, I like to prepare comfortable food. Yet I still want to express my appreciation for their friendship by putting a little extra effort into the meal. The seafood strudel can be cooked in advance, cooled, cut, and placed on a nonstick baking sheet to be reheated just before serving. The sauce could also be reheated, on top of the stove on medium heat.

The pork chops could be stuffed, seared, and ready to be popped into the oven. The potatoes can be cooked and left in water. Even the garlic could be prebaked. And, of course, the entire dessert could be made the day before and left in the freezer.

SHRIMP, SCALLOPS & SALMON STRUDEL
with a Champagne Mustard Sauce (*page 56*)

SMOKED HAM & CREAM CHEESE-STUFFED PORK CHOPS (*page 178*)

ROASTED-GARLIC MASHED POTATOES (*page 200*)

FROZEN LEMON & ORANGE SOUFFLÉ
with Lime & Yogurt Sauce (*page 230*)

glossary of chef's

sweat

You may wonder what I mean when I say "sweat the shallots." Quite simply, it means to cook a vegetable over medium heat until it softens and releases moisture, allowing it to blend quickly with other ingredients. This technique is especially necessary for dishes that require only a few minutes of cooking.

brunoise

This is a fancy word that simply means a small dice, approximately $1/8$-inch square. But remember, before you can make a brunoise, you must first make a julienne. What's that, you ask? Julienne means to cut in a long, thin strip. For example, if you cut long $1/8$-inch strips of bell pepper then cut those strips into $1/8$-inch squares, you will have a fine brunoise. Not so complicated!

chiffonade

This refers to an easy method for cutting fresh herbs and vegetable leaves into thin strips, like ribbons. For a fine chiffonade, roll the leaves very tightly into a cigar shape, then cut every $1/16$ inch. When you unroll the leaf, you will have a very thin strip that is wonderful as a garnish on top of salads and many other dishes. I use basil chiffonade quite often.

vocabulary

concassé

Tomato concassé is tomatoes that have been peeled and seeded. Why take the time to peel and seed a tomato, you ask? A tomato is like any other fruit—its skin would become chewy and its seeds would become hard during cooking. Just boil the tomatoes for 10 to15 seconds, and then plunge them into ice water immediately to stop the cooking process. Then cut the tomatoes into quarters—this makes it easy to peel and seed them.

coulis

This is a simple purée of vegetables or fruit. Usually I will add a small amount of chicken stock to make a savory coulis, and perhaps a small amount of liquor or fruit juice to make a fruit coulis. A food processor or blender makes this quick and easy to prepare.

dice

Not to be confused with brunoise, dices are small cubes of vegetables. A small dice is approximately $1/4$ inch, medium is $1/3$ inch, and a large dice is $3/4$ inch. Let's not get out the tape measure, though; unless otherwise specified, a $1/2$-inch dice works fine with most recipes.

julienne

Vegetables or fruit cut into thin strips from $1/8$ to $3/4$ inch. This step always precedes dicing.

blanch

This simple technique is crucial for protecting the color, texture, and flavor of such vegetables as green beans, carrots, broccoli, or cauliflower; it keeps them tender and delicious. Of course, every vegetable does not become tender to the bite in the same amount of time. The important thing to remember is that the moment it does, it should be plunged immediately in ice water to stop the cooking process, which will protect and enhance the color. Drain and preserve until needed.

roast a bell pepper

There are few things as wonderful as a freshly roasted pepper. And it's so easy to do! Place the pepper on an open gas burner until the skin blisters and turns completely black. Or, roast the pepper on a grill or under the broiler in the oven. Transfer it to a plastic bag, close it securely, and let it steam for 20 minutes. Scrape off the charred skin, then remove the stems and seeds. Try to avoid rinsing the pepper, as this will wash away too much of the roasted flavor. After the skin has been peeled, cut into julienne.

index

acknowledgments

First of all, I would like to thank my wonderful crew at The Left Bank who have diligently kept up our high standards as one of America's finest restaurants, while I have been busy tasting recipes, writing this book, and shooting an entirely new PBS television series. I am particularly grateful to Jacky Michot, my friend, Pastry Chef, and hardworking associate. Thank you for your good sense of humor and continued loyalty. To my assistant and secretary, Darlene Sadlo, thank you for your never-ending support.

Also, I want to thank the entire team at Time Life who has worked with such efficiency and have made this book twice as much fun to publish as my first book. I am eternally grateful to Terry Newell for his vote of confidence. A big "Thank-You" to the lovely Quentin McAndrew who discovered my project and decided to make this book a reality; thanks for your outstanding work ethic. My thanks to Jennifer Lee whom I talked to constantly; thank you for your patience and continuous support. Thanks to Michelle Murphy for her ability to sift through hours of tapes and for her great writing. And thanks to all the other talents at Time Life who have worked on this book to make it such an outstanding product of which I am very proud!

Thanks to my close friend, Doug Castanedo, whose great talents with the camera have allowed him to capture my food exactly as it was prepared, without coloring or any other trick photography.

I also want to acknowledge the entire cast of characters at WLRN, Channel 17, in Miami. Thanks to Joe Jabaly, my longtime friend and extraordinary producer. Without his creative talents the cooking show may never have become a reality. My gratitude goes to Angel Hernandez, the Director of Production; thanks for your patience and great sense of humor. Thanks also to all the camera operators, the set designer and the dozens of people who were involved in the production and editing of the show. I am especially grateful to Patricia Combine and Gustavo Sagastumne, the Executive Producers of the show, for the confidence they have shown in me.

Last but not least, I would like to express my fond appreciation to all my friends and customers at The Left Bank who always show such enthusiasm and lend great support to me in all my varied projects!